The Apricot

Microcomputer Handbooks

The
APRICOT

Peter Gosling

Pitman

Computer Handbooks

The complete list of titles in this series and the Pitman Pocket Guide series appears after the Index at the end of this Handbook. The Publishers would welcome suggestions for further additions and improvements to the series. Please write to Alfred Waller at the address given below.

Consultant Editor: David Hatter

PITMAN PUBLISHING LIMITED
128 Long Acre, London WC2E 9AN

Associated Companies
Pitman Publishing Pty Ltd, Melbourne
Pitman Publishing New Zealand Ltd, Wellington
Copp Clark Pitman, Toronto

© Peter Gosling 1985

First edition 1985

British Library Cataloguing in Publication Data

Gosling, Peter
  The apricot.—(Computer handbooks)
  1. ACT Apricot (Computer)
  I. Title   II. Series
  001.64'04   QA76.8.A/

ISBN 0 273 02317 9

Printed in Great Britain at the Pitman Press, Bath

Contents

Acknowledgements

The author wishes to record his thanks to Allan
Younger of Burghley Computers Ltd, Stamford, Steve
Green of Midland Micro Services, Stamford and
Brian Turner of CETAS Consultants Ltd, Holbeach for
their help in the preparation of this handbook.

How to Use this Handbook

This Handbook is a work of reference, not a textbook. It is designed as a quick and easy-to-use source of information about various aspects of the ACT Apricot microcomputer; its component parts and upgrades, the software supplied to all purchasers of the machine; and a concise overview of the way this software is used. It is not intended to be a comprehensive work of reference; nothing can replace the operating manuals in that field. It is often very difficult and confusing for the novice to find his way about a manufacturer's manual, however user friendly it attempts to be. Only when the topic covered by a manual has become familiar can it start being really useful. This Handbook aims to become a bridge between the new user and the manuals. It is arranged in such a way as to put all the components of the Apricot, both hardware and software, into their proper perspective and show how they relate to each other.

You will discover that some of the information in this Handbook differs from that given to you in the manuals supplied with your machine. This is because the software has been updated, but the manuals have not! The notes in here are prepared while using the latest version of the machine and its software.

A modern microcomputer such as the Apricot is a very sophisticated piece of electronics and it can be used successfully at a number of levels. It can be used purely as just another piece of office equipment, as part of a network of computers all talking to each other, or it can be used by a computer expert to develop new programs and systems. This Handbook is designed to be of value to a wide range of users.

Certain software is supplied as standard with all Apricot microcomputers. All models are delivered with an MS-DOS operating system, BASIC, the GSX graphics package, the SuperCalc spreadsheet, SuperWriter word processor and SuperPlanner diary/planner package. In addition, the F1 and Portable machines come with the ACT Diary diary/ planner, the ACT Sketch graphics package and ACT Game, described as 'a sophisticated executive pastime'! The Apricot Portable also features a speech recognition unit capable of responding to any set of 64 words selectable from a vocabulary of 4096.

Introducing the ACT Apricot

The ACT Apricot was first launched onto the market in October 1983. A 16-bit Intel 8086 microprocessor chip provides the processing power and 256K bytes of random access memory is provided as standard on the Portable, PC and XI models. The smallest model in the range, the Apricot F1, starts with a 128K byte RAM. Additional memory in the form of 128K byte, 256K byte or 512K byte expansion cards allows the RAM to be expanded.

Both the Apricot F1 and the Portable are supplied with a single floppy disk drive. The Apricot PC and XI models have one or two floppy disk drives and, if required, Winchester disks. The most powerful machines in the range are the Point 7 and Point 32 networking machines. Additional external Winchester disk drives can be fitted.

The smallest capacity disk storage available are on 315K (single-sided) or 720K byte (double-sided) floppy disk drive. Twin 315K and twin 720K floppy disk drives are also available. The disks are 3½ inch diameter by Sony and are housed in a hard plastic jacket fitted with a spring-loaded metal shutter which only opens after the disk has been loaded into the drive. They can be write-protected by a movable plastic tab in one corner and are considerably more robust than the more common 5¼ inch floppy disks in their flexible case.

The hard disks available for the Apricot are all of the popular and well-proven Winchester type and come in 5M byte or 10M byte sizes, when fitted in the unit, or in 5M byte, 10M byte or 15M byte sizes when supplied as an add-on unit external to the main unit.

The Apricot is unusual, but not unique, in that the keyboard contains a 2-line LED display, known as a microscreen, and as such can be folded up together with the disk drives to become a portable computer in its own right using the microscreen alone for the display. The microscreen is not supplied on the F1 or the Portable; their keyboards are arranged slightly differently from the others in the range. In fact, the Portable features a 25-line by 80-character liquid crystal display rather than a video screen. As the Apricot will work quite satisfactorily without a VDU screen this is treated by ACT as an optional extra. Various high-resolution monitors are available and it is possible to use the Apricot with a domestic TV set. Other extras supplied by ACT are an Intel 8087 arithmetic processor board for faster calculations, a 'mouse', a colour board for optional colour graphics and a modem board for communications over the public telephone network. Apricots can be networked with one machine acting as a fileserver to the others, including the other computer in the ACT range, the Sirius 1, on the network. The Portable is supplied with a speech recognition system.

Inside the main unit of the Apricot are the microprocessor and disk drives and, apart from its power supply socket, four sockets at the back. The keyboard is plugged into one of these. The others are a parallel printer port, a serial input/output port and a socket for the monitor screen.

The Apricot keyboard has 96 keys which include the usual typewriter keys, nine editing and cursor control keys, a numeric keypad with arithmetic function keys, eight labelled function keys and six touch-sensitive keys situated just below the microscreen. These keys assume various functions depending on the software being used at the time. Each key has a small red LED which is lit when the key is active. The function of the key is displayed above it on the microscreen. The 'Caps Lock' key operates on the alphabetic characters only leaving the numeric keys unaffected. The microscreen is powered by a battery which is contained in a compartment at the back of the keyboard. The keyboard also contains a connector for a 'mouse', the Reset button and the contrast control for the microscreen.

4

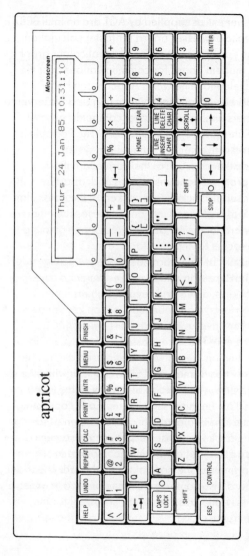

Apricot Keyboard

5

At the top of the keyboard are eight function keys which are labelled:

Help, **Undo**, **Repeat**, **Calc**, **Print**, **Intr**, **Menu**, **Finish**

The **Help** and **Finish** keys are used in conjunction with the ladder, which is described in the next section.

Undo cancels the last command entered.

Repeat repeats the last command entered.

Calc transfers control to the microscreen calculator so that the Apricot can be used as a desk calculator.

Print dumps the contents of the screen to the printer.

Intr interrupts whatever process is going on.

Menu returns you to a menu. Its action depends on the software being used at the time.

The LADDER

On starting the Apricot up the first thing the user sees is not the usual bland prompt provided by CP/M or MS-DOS. From the very beginning the operating system hands over to a program known as the 'Manager'. This presents the user with a menu from which a number of options can be chosen. These options are displayed on what ACT calls a 'Ladder', which is a series of boxes arranged as shown below. The first ladder is devoted to operating system utilities, the second to languages and the remainder to applications programs:

TOOLS	BASIC	WORD		
BACKUP	PASCAL	PLAN		
CONFIG		CALC		

FINISH

On the Apricot F1 the ladder is replaced with a series of 'Icons', representations of various operations, which are intended to be pointed to using the optional 'mouse'. The effect, however, is just the same as when the ladder feature is used.

These options can be changed and added to as you acquire more and more programs for your system. The manager and its ladder are more useful to those machines fitted with a Winchester hard disk, since all the programs can be stored in the one place. If only the 3½ inch floppy disks are fitted then the appropriate disk has to be loaded into a drive before the manager can call a program stored on it into memory.

A program selection is made from the manager by moving around the ladders using the cursor control keys. As the cursor is moved around, the names on the ladder are highlighted. At the same time the microscreen displays the names contained in the ladder where the highlight is located; each name being displayed above one of the touch-sensitive keys. A brief description of the highlighted program

7

appears at the bottom of the main screen. To enter your selection you have to move the cursor to the ladder where the program you require is located and press the touch-sensitive key beneath the name of the program required. For example, if "WORD" was highlighted a description such as:

"WORD" is the WORDSTAR word-processor

appears. To load WORDSTAR all that is needed is for you to touch the key immediately below "WORD" on the microscreen.

"HELP" is selected by moving the highlight to the HELP box and pressing RETURN, or by pressing the HELP key on the keyboard. FINISH is selected by depressing the FINISH key. These keys are situated at the ends of the top row on the Apricot keyboard. HELP will display information to supplement the contents of the manuals supplied by ACT to enable you to use the system more effectively. If "FINISH" is selected, then the manager will take you straight to the operating system, MS-DOS, and you will be given the MS-DOS prompt:

A>

If you wish to return to the manager from MS-DOS you simply have to type "MANAGER" and the ladder will appear.

The TOOLS option on the ladder will allow you to choose from a further ladder menu which looks like this:

The ALTER option allows you, among other things, to change the system date and time by choosing the CLOCK option from the next ladder menu. The date and time are displayed on the microscreen when the Apricot is switched on. The circuitry which maintains the date and time is controlled by the battery held within the keyboard. When CLOCK is chosen, another ladder appears and looks like this:

The touch-sensitive keys beneath the microscreen will have the words ACCEPT, HOUR, MIN, DAY, MONTH and YEAR displayed above them and when a key is touched the appropriate box is highlighted and hour, minute, day, month or year can be entered using the keys on the numeric pad. So when the screen looks like this, for example:

9

HELP			Set Time and Date	

ACCEPT
HOUR
MIN
DAY
MONTH
YEAR

		Hour	Min	
Time		15	10	
		Day	Month	Year
Date		07	10	1984

FINISH

the key beneath ACCEPT is touched and the time and
date are entered into the system. By touching the key
under FINISH you will be returned to the ladder
menu which brought you to the CLOCK ladder. Then
you have to press the FINISH key again to bring you
back to the TOOLS ladder. Finally, you press FINISH
yet again to return you to the MANAGER ladder. This
is necessary because of the tree structure of the
TOOLS commands. The DISK option gives you the
choice of a further menu containing:

HELP, DIR, CHANGE, BACKUP, FINISH

The ALTER menu provides you with the options of:

HELP, SERIAL, LIST, CLOCK, FINISH

The TAILOR menu gives options of:

HELP, EDITOR, FONT, KEYS, LOGO, OPTION,
FINISH

The CHANGE menu, reached via the DISK option, gives you the choice of:

HELP, COPY, RENAME, MATCH, DELETE, PNAME, FINISH

The BACKUP menu, reached also from DISK, gives the choice of:

HELP, FORMAT, COPY, VERIFY, SYSTEM, FINISH

The DIR option, reached from DISK, gives the choice of:

HELP, MAKE, PNAME, REMOVE, FINISH

What, in fact, TOOLS gives us is access to many MS-DOS utilities, but in a far more friendly manner.

The OPTION choice, reached from TOOLS via TAILOR, allows you to add new programs to the manager ladder and add a short description which is displayed when the program is selected.

Many of the options given from TOOLS will be familiar to you if you have used MS-DOS before. Those which are peculiar to the Apricot will be described in the MS-DOS section of this Handbook.

If the CONFIG option is chosen from the ladder you have the chance of modifying the operating system. As usual, you have a HELP option when you make this choice. CONFIG enables you to make changes in the logo which is displayed when the Apricot is powered up, the character set in use, the configuration of the keys so that special characters can be generated from the keyboard. Even the 'click' of the keys may be altered and the time you can hold a key down before it repeats. Also in the CONFIG routine is the capability of altering the data rates of the serial port, the number of stop bits, bits per character and other transmission characteristics.

When the BACK-UP selection is made from the ladder you are able to perform a number of operations on a disk. These are FORMAT, COPY, VERIFY and SYSTEM. FORMAT enables you to format a new disk, or reformat an old disk. COPY lets you copy the contents of one disk to another; VERIFY to check if the contents of two disks are identical and SYSTEM places an MS-DOS operating system onto the system tracks of a specified disk. (In order to make a freshly formatted disk 'bootable', copy the operating system onto it.)

If the **Calc** key is pressed, the Apricot calculator function is activated. Numbers are entered through the keypad at the right of the keyboard and they are displayed in the top left-hand corner of the microscreen. However, the calculator function is rather more than just a simple desk calculator.

It is very often that when producing text using a word-processor such as WORDSTAR we find the need to perform a calculation and enter the result into our text. This is done by first of all depressing the **Calc** key before loading the word-processing program. Then, at the point when the calculation is required, the **Calc** key is pressed and the calculation performed. One of the displays in the microscreen, second from the left, is "Send". Touch that key after the calculation has been completed and the result is sent straight to the screen to the current cursor position and neatly entered into your word-processed text.

Operating Systems for the Apricot

Note: When you first receive your Apricot system, get it into operation as described in the 'Getting Started' section of the Owner's Handbook. Press the "Finish" key and you will be presented with the

A>

prompt. If you then type the command "DIR" you will have the complete contents of the master disk displayed on the screen. To allow you to read this list before it disappears off the screen, press the "Stop" key. Press this again and scrolling will recommence. There will probably be a file on the disk called "READ.ME". Before going any further type:

A>TYPE READ.ME

and you will be given current information about the system you have been supplied with.

The above notes apply to both MS-DOS and CP/M-based operating systems.

MS-DOS

The standard operating system supplied with the Apricot is Version 2.00 of Microsoft's MS-DOS (Microsoft Disk Operating System) operating system. The main features of this version of the operating system are covered in the *Pocket Guide to MS-DOS*. Many of the utilities reached via the ladder are MS-DOS utilities, although sometimes they are known by slightly different names. For example, the TOOLS utility known as MAKE is MD or MKDIR in

MS-DOS. This is the utility which enables you to create new directories on the disk. A list of ladder utilities and their MS-DOS names are given below:

Utility	MS-DOS
MAKE	MKDIR or MD
PNAME	CHDIR or CD
REMOVE	RMDIR or RD
MATCH	DCOMP or DISKCOMP
CHECK	CHKDSK
CLOCK	TIME and DATE
EDITOR	EDLIN

In order to get directly to MS-DOS from the manager the FINISH option is chosen. To get back to the ladder:

A>MANAGER

is typed.

There are a number of special utilities for the Apricot which can be called from MS-DOS. They are:

KEYS   This allows you to load a different keyboard table into memory. KEYS followed by the saved table name will load the named keyboard table into memory. The previous table is saved under the name of KEYS.SAV. KEYS RESTORE brings the table saved under the name of KEYS.SAV back into memory. Only one previous key table can be saved.

FONT   This allows a new character font to be brought into use. Its use is very similar to the KEYS routine. The previous font is saved and a new named font is loaded into memory. Only one previous character font can be saved.

PRINTER   This directs the printer output to the serial or parallel port by:

A>PRINTER SERIAL

or

A>PRINTER PARALLEL

SETUP   This is the same as the CONFIG option chosen from the ladder.

MISCREEN   This allows you to control the microscreen and the touch-sensitive keys located beneath it.

MISCREEN CLOCK places the microscreen into calendar mode showing the date and time.

MISCREEN ECHO places the microscreen in a mode which allows it to display the last two lines displayed on the video screen.

MISCREEN KEY,X,Y,Z where X is a number in the range 1–6 (the function key numbers), Y is a six-character label, Z is a twelve-character command.

MISCREEN MESS allows you to display a 40-character message on the top line of the microscreen. It is of the form:

MISCREEN MESS, ''PITMAN HANDBOOK OF THE APRICOT''

SPOOLER   This utility allows you to place a number of files in a queue ready for the printer. It means that printing can be carried out while you are performing other tasks. It is used in conjunction with the MS-DOS utility called PRINT which adds files to the print queue.

BREAK   This enables or disables CONTROL-C, which usually terminates a program.
   BREAK ON disables CONTROL-C.
   BREAK OFF enables CONTROL-C.

EXIT   This is a batch command causing an exit from command level and a return to the previous level.

PAUSE   Suspends execution of a batch file. Press any key to continue.

PROMPT   This allows you to change the usual MS-DOS prompt of A>. For example, the prompt can be altered so that the current time together with some text is shown instead.

REM   This allows you to place comments into a batch file. The comment is displayed when the line is executed.

SET   Sets one string value equal to another for use in later commands or a batch file.

VER   Displays the Version number of the MS-DOS in use.

VOL   Displays the disk volume label.

A useful feature of MS-DOS is its ability to create a virtual disk in memory. You create, as far as MS-DOS is concerned, a new disk drive, of a size determined by you, within memory. It is treated exactly as if it was a normal disk drive with the added attraction of being able to have data read and written at very much higher speeds than if a real disk was being used. The only restriction on the use of this virtual disk is that it cannot retain what is written to it after the power has been switched off. The 'disk' is created by editing a system file called CONFIG.SYS, using either EDLIN or a word processor such as Wordstar or SuperWriter. By this means you insert an extra line in this file consisting of:

device=ramdisk.sys/n

where n is the number of 64K blocks of memory you wish to allocate to the 'disk'. If you have an Apricot with two floppy disks, or a Winchester disk and a single floppy disk, this new storage device becomes known as drive C. If you have a single floppy disk system it is known as drive B.

CP/M

Although the standard operating system for the Apricot is MS-DOS, purchasers of the machine have the chance of using a specially tailored version of CP/M on request. This is available free from ACT on the return of a card enclosed with the Apricot. The version of CP/M (Control Program for Microcomputers) supplied is CP/M-86+ which needs a minimum of 256K bytes of RAM in order to work effectively. It possesses all the features of the 8-bit CP/M Version 2.2 with a number of additions and changes. For example, files with the .COM extension have a .CMD extension in CP/M-86+. The assembler is known as ASM86.CMD and the dynamic debugging tool is known in this version as DDT86.CMD. In addition, the LOAD command of the 8-bit 2.2 version is replaced by GENCMD.CMD. This converts the output from ASM86, which has the .H86 extension, into an executable command file. A file presented to the assembler must have the .A86 extension. The command SHOW will give information regarding the status of the system as well as a list of the files on the directory. It is a combination of DIR and STAT.

A full description of the features of CP/M are to be found in the Pitman *Pocket Guide to CP/M*.

If you buy an Apricot fitted with a hard (Winchester technology) disk you will find that it is delivered with MS-DOS and all the accompanying software, SuperCalc, SuperPlanner and SuperWord, already on the disk. If you send off for your free CP/M-86+ and Concurrent CP/M-86 operating systems they will arrive on a set of five floppy disks. In this case what you need to do is to place your CP/M-86+ disk into the floppy disk drive and you will find that it will boot up into CP/M-86+. You will know this because the Digital Research logo is displayed at the top right-hand corner of the screen.

The CP/M disks do not contain the SuperCalc, SuperPlanner and SuperWord packages, but do contain a simplified version of BASIC language called 'Personal BASIC'. This latter program is designed to help you to learn to program in BASIC easily and quickly. However, you will discover that you can access programs on the hard disk even though they are MS-DOS programs. By this means you will be able to use MSBASIC, SuperCalc and SuperWriter without any difficulty. However, the author found that CP/M-86+ baulked at SuperPlanner for some reason!

A word of warning, however, about getting CP/M-86+ going on a hard disk Apricot. You need to look very carefully at the BIOS (Basic Input Output System) version number printed on the disk label. If you have been supplied with Version 2.3, then it will work on a hard disk system; Version 1.5, the alternative, will only work on an Apricot with floppy disk drives.

On loading CP/M-86+ into memory the first message to be displayed tells you the version number of the operating system and the copyright notice followed by a system description and then the familiar

A>

prompt.

If you need help regarding the use of CP/M-86+ there is a help facility which is reached by typing:

A>HELP

19

HELP followed by the command name for which help is required — HELP SHOW for example — will provide a page of information and examples of the use of that command. HELP DIR OPTIONS provides help on the DIR command and its options. On the latest version of CP/M-86+ seen by the author, the READ.ME file states that several utilities mentioned in HELP are not yet available. These are DEVICE, DUMP86, PATCH, BACK and GET.

CP/M-86+ offers a number of features available in neither CP/M-86 nor the more common 8-bit versions of the operating system. These are listed below:

COPYDISK   Copies the contents of a disk, track by track, onto a previously formatted disk. All tracks, including system tracks, are copied.

DATE   Allows you to set the date and time by entering:

A>DATE 12/12/84 12:00:00

The format of the date is MM/DD/YY and the time is HH:MM:SS.

A>DATE C   Causes the current date and time to be displayed continuously.

INITDIR   Before you can set date and time stamps onto the files in a directory, the directory has to be initialized by the INITDIR program.

PUT Directs system to put console or printer output to a file. The opposite of GET.

SET This provides for the use of passwords attached to certain files and directories, the selection of attributes for files and disk drives and date/time stamping of files. A file has a password attached to it by:

SET ASM86.CMD [PASSWORD=SNOOPY].

A file can be write protected and password protected at the same time by:

SET SECRET.TXT [PASSWORD = SNOOPY, PROTECT = WRITE]

A disk drive can be set to be read-only by:

SET B:[RO]

Date and time stamping can be applied to all subsequently created files by:

SET [CREATE = ON]

If ACCESS is set on, instead of CREATE, then when the SDIR command is issued the date and time of the last access made to that file is listed. If CREATE is set on the creation, date is listed. A disk can be named using the SET command by using NAME:

SET [NAME = SALLY'S.TXT]

A file can be write protected and password protected at the same time by:

SET SECRET.TXT [PASSWORD = SNOOPY, PROTECT = WRITE]

SHOW   The CP/M-86+ version of the more common STAT command but gives information as well about all the system resources, SHOW LABEL, SHOW SPACE, SHOW USERS and SHOW DRIVES. SHOW LABEL show the amount of space displays the directory labels, whether any passwords are required, the date and time stamps for the directories. SHOW SPACE is the same as SHOW on its own. SHOW USERS list the active users and the active files. SHOW DRIVES list the drive characteristics, number of records, number of bytes used and free.

STOP   This halts a background program.

USER   CP/M-86+ allows a number of different areas of the disk drives to be assigned to various users; these users are assigned numbers, 0–15, by the USER command. USER 1 changes the user number and causes the prompt to become:

1A>

It also puts user 1 into a directory specific to that user.

Concurrent CP/M

The third operating system available for the Apricot is Concurrent CP/M-86. Like the CP/M-86+ operating system this is obtained free on request from ACT. The same comments as were made about the use of CP/M-86+ apply to Concurrent CP/M-86. You should note, however, that at least 384K bytes of

RAM are needed in order for Concurrent CP/M-86 to work.

Concurrent CP/M-86 controls up to four separate jobs running at any one time and the results are displayed on four 'virtual consoles'. The progress of the four independent jobs can be viewed at any time by displaying any one of the four virtual consoles. However attractive Concurrent CP/M appears, you must realize that it can do no more than the machine is capable of. Do not expect to be able to run four large applications programs at the same time. This is because you may not have enough memory to store all four programs at once, because that is what is needed. Even two BASIC programs will not run in a 512K byte machine under Concurrent CP/M-86. This is because each program requires the BASIC interpreter to be resident in its portion of memory.

The consoles are numbered 0, 1, 2 and 3 and because each console can be treated as a separate machine running programs under its own CP/M operating system, all the usual CP/M commands are available. On loading Concurrent CP/M-86 a message is displayed similar to the one shown when CP/M-86+ is loaded. It consists of a banner proclaiming the version number and copyright notice followed by a display showing the system configuration.

Beneath this will be a prompt similar to that of the more familiar CP/M, except that it always consists of a number followed by the drive letter. Initially this will be:

0A>

To switch from one 'console' to another all that is needed is for you to press Ctrl-0, 1, 2 or 3. At the bottom of the screen is the 'status line' giving information about the current state of the system.

Commands which are specific to Concurrent CP/M-86 are:

ABORT   This stops execution of a named program running at any one of the consoles. The program name can be followed by the number of the console where the program is running. If a program is aborted from the console which started it, the program must be DETACHed first.

CONFIG   This command allows you to configure the system to support up to five printers connected to your system. The configuration allows you to set baud rate, word length, parity and stop bits on any port.

DSKRESET   If a change of disk is required, then this command is used. If a program running on any one of the consoles is using the disk in question, then reset is denied. The command is used both before and after the change of disk.

ERAQ   This is similar to the usual CP/M ERA command except that each instruction to erase a file is queried.

PRINTER   This command allows a user to specify which printer is to be used for output by following the command with the printer number, set by CONFIG.

SDIR   This gives you information about the files in any directory and for any user. For example, SDIR[USER = ALL] will list the contents of the directories for all users. It also provides information about the size of the files and the disk space left.

SYSDISK   Shows the current system disk in use.

USER   In Concurrent CP/M-86 the user number is also the virtual console number. Although up to sixteen users can be specified, only four can actively be running programs.

VCMODE   This changes the operating mode of a virtual console. A console can be either DYNAMIC or BUFFERED. If a virtual console is BUFFERED it will create a full screen and then suspend processing until that screen has been displayed. If DYNAMIC has been chosen the screen changes as data is output to it even though it has not been displayed. Also, this command can be used to set the maximum file size to be available to that console by:

VCMODE size = 10

which sets the maximum file size for that console to be 10K bytes. This can only be done when the console is in BUFFERed mode. The VCMODE command is always entered from the appropriate console.

One particular CP/M command which has an extension for use under both CP/M-86+ and Concurrent CP/M-86 is the PIP command. Because Concurrent CP/M-86 allows a series of user areas to be set up, PIP has to be able to move files not only between disks but also between user areas. This is achieved by putting a user number prefixed by the letter G after the source file or destination file name. This means that by typing:

PIP FILE1[G1]=FILE2[G2]

the file called FILE1 in user area 1 is PIPped from a file called FILE2 in user area 2.

MS-BASIC

In the version of BASIC supplied with the Apricot, Version 5.23 of BASIC-86, the 16-bit version of BASIC, variable names can be of any length of which the first 40 characters are significant. A variable cannot bear a name which is one of the BASIC keywords as listed in the following pages. Variable types are:

String variables   names which terminate in a $ sign. Can contain anything from zero (null string) to 255 characters.

T$,JOHN$,A0$,COMPANY$

Arrays of numerics or strings   must include subscripts in parentheses.

A$(3,4),TOTAL(4),NUMBER(J,K,L)

26

Integers names which terminate in a % sign. Must be in the range −32768 to +32767; occupy two bytes of memory.

FLAG%,H%,BASE%

Single-precision variables names which terminate in the ! sign; occupy four bytes of memory.

A!,TOTAL!,BALANCE!,R0!

Double-precision variables names which terminate in the # sign; occupy eight bytes of memory.

B#,MICRO#,G7#

Any variable name which has no terminating character \$, %, ! or # is considered to be a single-precision variable.

Single-precision numeric constants any number which contains seven or less digits or is in exponential form using E or terminates with !.

3.4567,−2.3E27,5678.897777!

Double-precision numeric constants any number which contains more than seven digits or is in exponential form using D or terminates with #.

−3.45623D−3,3.50#,6787970.3456

Hexadecimal numbers Have the prefix &H.

&HFFF,&H100,&H001

Octal numbers have the prefix &O.

&O001,&O777,&O456

Order of execution of BASIC arithmetic:

1. Brackets
2. Exponentiation ^ sign
3. Multiplication and division / sign
4. Integer division \ sign
5. MOD
6. Addition and subtraction

Operations in parentheses are performed first.
Equal precedence operations are performed from
left to right.

 In the following examples many of the BASIC
statements given are followed by a single quote
mark—'—this is the equivalent of the word REM,
REMark, which is a comment entered for explanatory
purposes only.

ABS   Returns the absolute value of a numeric
expression.

```
10   X=2.3:X1=−1
20   Y=ABS(X)
30   Z=ABS(X*X1)   'Stores 2.3 in both Z and Y
```

ASC   Returns the ASCII code for the first character
of a string.

```
10   X$="BILL"
20   X=ASC(X$)   'Stores 66 in X
```

ATN   Returns the arctangent (in radians, not degrees) of a numeric expression.

```
10   P=3.09
20   Q=ATN(P)   'Stores 1.257809 in Q
```

AUTO   Sets automatic line numbering into operation. Unless otherwise instructed, AUTO will start numbering at 10 and proceed in increments of 10. Saves you having to type line numbers in. AUTO is terminated by Ctrl C.

AUTO 50,5

First line is line 50, line numbers increment in units of five.

BLOAD   Will load a memory image file into memory. The arguments are the filename and an optional offset, which must be in the range 0 to 65535. The offset is the address where loading is to start.

BLOAD CUBE,0   'Where CUBE is the filename and
               0 is the number of bytes offset
               from the last DEF SEG statement.
               If the offset is not specified, then
               the loading takes place at the
               location it was saved from

29

BSAVE   Will save a section of memory to a named file, with a specified offset and with a specified length. The form of a BSAVE command is:

BSAVE,filename,offset,length
  'All three parameters must be specified. The offset is the segment specified in the last DEF SEG statement

CALL   Will call a machine code subroutine. The form of a CALL is:

10   CALL X,(V1,V2, ...)
    'Where X is a numeric variable specifying the starting address of the subroutine being called, as an offset from the last DEF SEG statement. The optional variables in brackets are parameters passed to the subroutine

CDBL   Will convert a numeric variable into a double-precision number.

```
10   X=2.95
20   PRINT(CDBL(X))   'Will print
                         2.949999809265137
```

CHAIN   Calls another program into memory. Passes variables from one program to the other. Can be used together with MERGE in order to use overlays. One extension to the command is ALL which allows all the variables in the calling program to be used in the final program — otherwise a COMMON statement is needed. Another extension is DELETE which deletes lines in the calling program not needed by the overlaid program.

```
790   CHAIN "PROG3"   'Loads and runs program
                              "PROG3"
800   CHAIN MERGE "PROG4"
      'Merges "PROG4" with the existing program.
      "PROG4" must have been saved in ASCII
      form
810   CHAIN MERGE "PROG5",500
      'Merges program "PROG5" and commences
      execution at line 500
820   CHAIN "PROG6",ALL
      'Chains "PROG6" and transfers all variables
      to the new program
830   CHAIN MERGE "PROG7",500,DELETE 500–
      1000
      'Deletes lines 500 through 1000 of the calling
      program before the chaining takes place
840   CHAIN MERGE "PROG8",750,ALL,DELETE
      750–1250
```

COMMON   Lists the variables which are common to two programs; should form part of both programs. Arrays and lists in COMMON should have () after their names. COMMON is best declared at the start of a program.

```
10    DIM A(25,100)
20    COMMON A(),X,Y,A$
```

CVI   Converts string variables into numeric integer variables. Used when reading data from a random file buffer.

```
100   FIELD #2,10 AS A$,2 AS P$
110   GET#2,1:P=CVI(P$)
```

CVS   As above, but for single-precision numbers.

```
100   FIELD #3,25 AS N$,4 AS S$
110   GET#3,1:S=CVS(S$)
```

CVD   As above, but for double-precision numbers.

```
100   FIELD #4,20 AS C$,8 AS D$
110   GET #4,1:D=CVD(D$)
```

CHR$ Returns the character represented by the ASCII decimal code specified in the argument.

```
10   PRINT CHR$(66)   'Will print the character "B"
```

CINT   Returns the integer value of a numeric expression by rounding.

```
10   PRINT CINT(3.456)   'Prints the number 3
20   PRINT CINT(-3.456)   'Prints the number -3
30   PRINT CINT(-2.9)   'Prints -3
```

CLEAR   Will set all numeric variables to zero and all strings to nulls. Can be used to set the end of memory and the amount of stack space.

```
CLEAR   'Clears memory
CLEAR ,32768   'Clears memory and sets memory
                 size to 32768 bytes
CLEAR ,,1000   'Clears memory and allocates 1000
                 bytes to the stack
CLEAR ,32768,1000   'Clears memory, sets memory
                       size and allocates 2000 bytes
                       to the stack
```

Note the commas in the commands.

32

CLOSE   Closes any input/output device or file
previously OPENed.

```
1000    CLOSE#1    'Closes file on Channel 1
1010    CLOSE2     'Closes file on Channel 2. The # is
                     optional
1020    CLOSE      'Closes all open files
```

CONT   Resumes execution of the program after the
program has been interrupted by CONTROL-C,
END or STOP instructions in the program.
   If the program has been edited after it stopped you
will get the "Can't continue" message. If you wish to
continue the program you can type "GOTO xxxx",
where xxxx is any line number.

COS   The trigonometric cosine of the argument
(which must be in radians, not degrees).

```
10    X=3.141593
20    C=COS(X)    'Stores the number −1 in C
```

CSNG   Converts the number stored under the
specified variable name into a single-precision
number.

```
10    A#=9999999.99999#
20    PRINT A#,CSNG(A#)
      'Will print 9999999.99999   1E+07
```

DATA   Must prefix a data list accessed by a READ
statement.

```
1000    DATA 100,"10,Mornington Crescent",
        Harry,&H00FA
```

DATE$ is a 10-character string variable of the form MM/DD/YYYY. It may have been set by the operating system prior to use of BASIC.

```
100   PRINT DATE$
      'Will print, for example, "01-31-1984"
110   DATE$="1/31/82"
      'Will be stored by padding out as above
```

DEF FN Defines a function used within the program. FN is followed by a name for the function and by its definition.

```
100   DEF FNCASH(P,T,R)=P*T*R/100
110   INPUT PRINCIPAL,TIME,RATE
120   INTEREST=FNCASH(PRINCIPAL,TIME,RATE)
130   PRINT INTEREST
      'Use the function defined in line 100 to
       calculate interest
```

DEF SEG Defines a segment of memory. The use of the BLOAD, BSAVE, CALL, PEEK, POKE or USER commands will define the actual address used as an offset into this segment. If no parameter is specified, then the segment to be used is set to the BASIC data segment (DS). The parameter value must lie between 0 and 65535.

```
10    DEF SEG=&HB800
```

DEFINT, DEFSNG, DEFDBL, DEFSTR   Define a
variable or variables to be of a particular type.

10	DEFINT I–N	'Defines all variables beginning with the letters I through N as integers — hence the % is not needed
20	DEFSNG P,Q	'Defines all variables whose names begin with P or Q to be of single-precision type — hence the ! sign is not needed
30	DEFDBL D,X–Z	'Defines all variables whose names begin with D or X through Z to be of double-precision type — hence the # is not needed
40	DEFSTR S	'Defines all names beginning with S to be of string type — hence the $ is not needed

Any names which terminate in the %, !, #, $
characters override any DEF statement.

DEF USR   Defines the starting address of a machine
code subroutine.

```
100   DEF SEG = 0
110   DEF USR3=32000
      'Defines the starting address of routine USR3,
      offset from location zero, i.e. its absolute
      address is 32000
120   Y=USR3(Q)
```

The number following USR can be any in the range 0
through 9.

DELETE   Deletes lines from a program.

DELETE 400   'Deletes line 400
DELETE 1000–2000   'Deletes all lines numbered
                              1000 through 2000
DELETE –100   'Deletes all lines up to and including
                    line 100

DIM   Defines the range of array subscripts.

10   DIM A(100,100),SIZE$(150),POS(X,Y,Z)

Unless otherwise specified by OPTION BASE all
arrays will have an element with subscript 0. The
maximum number of dimensions allowed is 255; the
maximum number of elements per dimension is
32767. If an array variable is used in a program, then
a maximum of ten elements per dimension is allowed
without a DIM statement.

EDIT   Used to edit the contents of a line of BASIC
program.

EDIT xxx   'Will call the line with number xxx into the
                edit buffer ready for editing
EDIT.   'Will place the current line into the edit
            buffer. Move the cursor to the appropriate
            place in the line using the Space Bar to move
            the cursor to the right, or the Rubout key to
            move it to the left

When in EDIT mode the line number is displayed and
the cursor is placed at the first character of the line
after the line number.

36

To insert characters, press I followed by the required additional characters. Insertion is ended by depression of the Escape key.

To add characters at the end of a line of BASIC, press X and type in the additional characters. Press Return to end the addition.

To delete characters, press D preceded by the number of characters to be deleted. For example, 6D will delete the six characters from the current cursor position.

To delete all the characters from the right of the cursor position, press H. You can then insert extra characters if required.

To search for a particular character, press S followed by the character searched for. This will stop the cursor at the first occurrence of the character. To find the third occurrence of the character 'L' in the line, enter 3SL.

To delete all the characters up to a certain point in the line, press K followed by the character. For example, 2KL will delete all the line up to the second occurrence of the letter 'L'.

To change the character following the cursor position to another character, press C followed by the new character. For example, CT will change the next character from whatever it is into the letter 'T'.

Pressing the Return key will print the rest of the line and replace the previous line with the edited line.

Press E to exit from the editor without printing the rest of the line.

Pressing L will cause the rest of the line to be printed and places the cursor at the start of the line. The line can then be re-edited.

Press A to abort the editing process. The original line is displayed and the cursor placed at the beginning of the line.

Press Q to quit the editor and return to BASIC. No editing changes will be saved.

If CONTROL-A is pressed while you are typing a line, a '!' character is displayed and the cursor goes to the start of the line.

If you want to copy a line to another line so that, for example, a complicated formula is repeated at another point of the program with another line number, type EDIT xxxx, where xxxx is the line number of the line to be copied. Then press E, for Edit, and follow this by CONTROL-A. A '!' character is printed. Press I, for Insert, and type a new line number. Press Return and the line is displayed with its new line number. For example, if you have:

```
100   X = SQR(A ^ 2 + B ^ 2)
```

Type 'EDIT 100' and then CONTROL-A. You will get:

```
!
```

Then press I and type '200' followed by Return. You will get:

```
! 200 X = SQR(A ^ 2 + B ^ 2)
```

Type 'LIST' and you will get:

```
100   X = SQR(A ^ 2 + B ^ 2)
200   X = SQR(A ^ 2 + B ^ 2)
```

If BASIC finds a syntax error in your program it will stop execution of the program, enter EDIT mode and display the line number of the line in error.

END   Will stop the program and close all files.

2500   END   'Does not have to be the last program
                  statement

EOF   Refers to an end of file marker. If an end of
file marker is found, then EOF is set to 'True', i.e. −1.
Otherwise it is set to 'False', i.e. 0. Only relevant to
serial files.

```
50   IF EOF(1) THEN GOTO 90
60   INPUT#1,A,B,C
70   PRINT A,B,C
80   GOTO 50   'Note how this takes you to the EOF
                     test and then the next file input
                     statement, not the other way round
90   END
```

ERASE   Clears any arrays from a program. Useful if
you want to redimension arrays during the course of
a program.

```
200   ERASE A$,B,TOTALS
```

ERR and ERL   ERR is the numerical error code for the
last error encountered. ERL returns the line where the
error occurred. Useful for error trapping by using
the ON ERROR command:

```
10   ON ERROR GOTO 100
20   FOR I=1 TO 3
30   READ X(I)
40   NEXT I
50   STOP
60   DATA 3,4
100  IF ERR=4 THEN PRINT "OUT OF DATA —
     BUT CARRY ON":RESUME 120
120  PRINT "HELP"
```

or

```
10   ON ERROR GOTO 100
100  PRINT "Error No:";ERR;"At line "; ERL
```

ON ERROR GOTO 0 will disable the error trapping routine.

ERROR   Simulates an error in BASIC; also useful for locating errors defined by you. Must have a parameter between 0 and 255.

```
500  ERROR 27     'Will cause the "Paper out"
                   message to be printed
```

or

```
10   ON ERROR GOTO 100
20   INPUT "PASSWORD";P$
30   IF P$<>"SNOOPY" THEN ERROR 99
40   STOP   'The rest of the program can follow
             here
100  IF ERR=99 THEN PRINT "WRONG
     PASSWORD"
110  IF ERL=30 THEN RESUME 20
```

EXP   Returns the exponential function.

```
10   X=2.4
20   PRINT EXP(X)   'Prints 11.02318
```

FIX   Will convert any floating point number into an integer by truncation.

```
10   PRINT FIX(2.34)   'Prints 2
20   PRINT FIX(-2.34)   'Prints -2
```

FIELD   Used to define the size and allocation of strings in the buffer for a random access file. All fields in a random file must be strings and conversion of numerics by MKI$, MKS$ and MKD$ must take place before a record is placed in such a file.

```
10   OPEN "R",#2,"RFILE,35
20   FIELD #2,20 AS A$,10 AS B$,5 AS C$
```

FILES   Lists the filenames of those files, program or data, which are stored on disk.

```
FILES   'Lists all files present
FILES "*.DAT"   'Lists all files with .DAT extension
```

Uses 'wildcards' in the same way as MS-DOS.

GET   Gets a specified record from a random file. Places it into the buffer.

```
250   GET#1,15   'Gets the 15th record from file #1.
                  If the record number is omitted,
                  the next record is read
```

FOR/NEXT   Sets up a program loop defining the
number of times the instructions in the loop are to be
executed.

FOR Startvalue of variable TO Targetvalue STEP
increment
   Body of loop
NEXT variable

If the increment is omitted it is taken to be 1.

```
10    FOR I = 1 TO 10 STEP 0.5
20    PRINT I ^ 2    'Prints the values of
                        1 ^ 2,1.5 ^ 2,2 ^ 2 . . . 10 ^ 2
30    NEXT I
```

FOR/NEXT loops can be nested one within
another.
   You can test how a FOR/NEXT works by running
the following program:

```
10    INPUT S,F,I    'Use test values of 1,10,1 then
                         1,1,1 and then 2,1,1
20    FOR V = S TO F STEP I
30    PRINT V;
40    NEXT
50    PRINT "FINAL VALUE OF V ";V
```

FRE   Returns the number of bytes of memory
available to your program at that point. Must be
followed by a dummy argument. If the argument is a
dummy string, then all the spare string space is
collected up into useful string space.

```
1000   PRINT FRE(0)
1010   PRINT FRE(" ")      'Both of these return the
                           same number of bytes but
                           the second collects up the
                           garbage first
```

GOSUB/RETURN   Interrupts program flow to execute a subroutine at specified line number. On encountering RETURN jumps back to statement following the original GOSUB.

```
 100   GOSUB 2000
 110   STOP   'Rest of program would be here
2000   PRINT "HERE WE ARE AT LINE 2000"
2010   RETURN
```

GOTO   Unconditional jump statement to cause execution to be transferred to the instructions starting at the specified line number.

```
500   GOTO 1000   'Next instruction executed is on
                  line 1000
```

HEX$ Returns the hexadecimal value of a decimal number in string form. The number must be in the range −32768 to 65535.

```
150   X=100
160   H$=HEX$(X)   'Sets H$ to be "64"
```

IF/THEN/ELSE   Allows conditional branching to
take place on the result of evaluating the truth or
otherwise of the IF statement.

```
10   INPUT X
20   IF X< 10 THEN PRINT "SMALL" ELSE PRINT
       "LARGE"
```

The instruction following the THEN and the ELSE can
be any valid BASIC instruction. You cannot use an IF
statement which looks like this:

```
500   IF 1<X<10 THEN PRINT "IN RANGE"
```

The ELSE clause is optional. IF statements can be
used in conjunction with AND, OR and NOT
conjunctions. For example:

```
750   IF X<10 AND X>1 THEN PRINT "IN RANGE"
800   IF X>10 OR X<1 THEN PRINT "OUT OF
        RANGE"
```

An expression such as

```
900   IF K THEN 1000
```

tests to see if K is zero or non-zero. Only if K is
non-zero (True) then the jump to line 1000 is made.
The truth or otherwise of a statement is determined
by the values of the 'logical' operators in the
program. A value of 0 indicates a false condition
whereas a non-zero value indicates truth.
   Try this simple program to see how it works:

```
10   FOR K=−3 TO 3
20   IF K THEN PRINT K;" TRUE"
       ELSE PRINT K;" FALSE"
30   NEXT K
```

Similarly

910 IF NOT K THEN 2000

will only jump to 2000 if NOT(K) is true, i.e. if K has any value such that NOT K is non-zero.

This program illustrates how this works:

```
10   FOR K=-3 TO 3
20   IF NOT K THEN PRINT K;" TRUE"
     ELSE PRINT K;" FALSE"
30   NEXT K
```

If both operands are 0 or −1, then the logical operators return 0 or −1, i.e. NOT(0) is −1 and NOT(−1) is 0.

INKEY$ Reads one character from the keyboard. A program segment which waits for any key to be pressed before carrying on is:

```
100   KB$=INKEY$
110   IF KB$=" " THEN 100
```

Or if you want to wait for a specific key to be pressed:

```
100   KB$=INKEY$
110   IF KB$=" " THEN 100
120   IF KB$<>"B" THEN 100
```

INKEY$ does not require the ENTER key to be pressed.

INP   Returns a byte from a specified port. The port number must be in the range 0 to 65535.

100   X=INP(255)   'Reads a byte from port 255 into variable X

INPUT   Stores the input from the keyboard in a list of named variables.

10   INPUT X,Y,A$

A prompt string can be included in the statement:

20   INPUT "Type in your name ";NAME$

INPUT#   Reads data from a device or a file and stores the data in specified program variables. The file must have been OPENed in the correct mode for this to take place.

200   INPUT#2,A,B,C$

INPUT$ Similar to INKEY$: the keyboard response is not echoed and RETURN is not needed. It can be used for accepting only certain characters as input:

10   PRINT "TYPE IN THE PASSWORD"
20   X$=INPUT$(6)
      'The argument is the number of characters
       accepted
30   IF X$="SNOOPY" THEN 1000 ELSE 10

Input can be accepted from a specified file if its channel number is specified and the file has already been opened in the correct mode.

50   S$=INPUT$(6,#1)

46

INSTR Searches a named string for the first occurrence of a test string.

```
500   EXAMPLE$="CAMBRIDGE"
510   TEST$="M"
520   PRINT INSTR(EXAMPLE$,TEST$)   'Prints 3
```

If you write INSTR(n,A$,B$) you will force the search to start after the nth character in A$.

INT Returns the largest integer less than or equal to the argument.

```
10   X=INT(4.3)    'Stores 4 in X
20   Y=INT(-4.3)   'Stores -5 in Y
```

KILL Deletes a named file from disk.

```
KILL "PROG1"
100   KILL "A:DATA1"   'Deletes file "DATA1" from
                        the disk in drive A
```

LEFT$ Locates the leftmost n characters of a string.

```
450   D$=LEFT(A$,10)   'Stores the first ten
                        characters of A$ in D$
```

LEN Returns the length of (i.e. number of characters in) a string.

```
200   K = LEN(A$)    'Stores the number of
                      characters in A$ in K
```

47

LET The assignment keyword. Assigns the value of the variable on the right of the = sign to the variable on its left. The right-hand side can be an expression.

```
10   LET X = 6.89
20   LET Y = X
30   LET Z = X ^ 2 − 3*Y + 4.567   'LET is optional
```

LINE INPUT and LINE INPUT# Reads a string containing commas into a variable or a file record.

```
100   LINE INPUT A$   'Would read a string such as
                            "17,Main St" into A$
200   LINE INPUT#2,A$   'Would read "17,Main St"
                            from next record of serial
                            file #2
```

LIST Lists BASIC statements of current program in memory.

```
LIST 200   'Lists line 200 only
LIST 200–300   'Lists all lines 200 through 300
LIST 200–   'Lists all lines from 200 to the end
LIST –200   'Lists all lines up to and including 200
LIST 100–300,"filename"   'Lists to "filename" all
                            listing is done in ASCII
```

LLIST As above, but to the line printer exclusively.

LOAD Loads a specified BASIC program into memory.

```
LOAD "MAIL"   'Loads program "MAIL" into
                  memory
LOAD "MAIL",R   'Loads and runs program "MAIL"
```

LOC Returns current position of the file pointer. It is the record number of the last record read from a random file or the number of records read so far from a serial file.

```
500   IF LOC(2)=75 THEN GOSUB 1400
      'Tests to see if it has read the 75th record from
       the file
```

LOF Returns the length of a file in bytes.

```
450   N=LOF(4) 'Stores number of bytes taken up
                 by file 4 in N
```

LOG Returns the natural logarithm of the argument.

```
180   X = 3.4 : L=LOG(X)  'Stores 1.223775 in L
```

LPOS Returns the current position of the printer print head in the print buffer.

```
135   H = LPOS(0)
      'Stores the current position of print head, in
       number of characters, in H
```

LPRINT and LPRINT USING Directs the output to the printer instead of the screen.

```
150   LPRINT "The total is :";TOTAL
```

LSET Left justifies a string in its field in the random file buffer.

```
40   FIELD #2,20 AS A$,15 AS B$
50   N$="PETER":LSET A$=N$
```

MERGE   Merges the contents of an ASCII file held
on backing store with the current program held in
memory. Equivalent to entering new program lines
from the keyboard.

MERGE "NEWFILE"

MID$ Returns a portion of a specified string.

```
600   P$=MID$(A$,4,2)      'Stores the substring of A$
                            which is two characters
                            long, starting with the
                            fourth character, in P$
```

MKI$ Converts a number into a string integer
expression prior to storage in a record of a random
file.

MKS$ As above for conversion into a string single-
precision expression.

MKD$ As above for conversion into a string
double-precision expression.

```
40   FIELD #2,2 AS I$,4 AS S$,8 AS D$
50   INPUT I,S,D
60   LSET I$=MKI$(I)
70   LSET S$=MKS$(S)
80   LSET D$=MKD$(D)
```

NAME Changes the name of a file. Similar to RENAME in MS-DOS.

```
10  NAME "PROG1" AS "PROG2"
    'Changes the name of the first file to that
     following AS
```

NEW Deletes program currently in memory.

NULL Sets the number of nulls to be printed at the end of every line.

```
NULL 3   'Prints 3 nulls at the end of every line
```

OCT$ Returns the octal (Base 8) value of a decimal number in string form.

```
20  O$ = OCT$(10)   'Stores "12" in O$
```

ON ERROR, ON/GOSUB, ON/GOTO Direct program flow to specified lines of BASIC program depending on certain conditions being fulfilled.

```
 10  ON ERROR GOTO 500   'If an error condition
                          occurs, go to line
                          500
100  ON K GOTO 200,300,400
     'If K = 1 go to line 200, if K = 2 go to line 300, if
     K = 3 go to line 400. Otherwise go to next
     statement
300  ON J GOSUB 600,700,800
     'As above but subroutines executed
```

OPEN   Opens a channel to or from a file on the
current backing store. This command is available in
two forms.

(1) OPEN "filename" FOR mode AS # filenum LEN
    = reclen

where the mode is OUTPUT,INPUT or APPEND (disk
files only) the reclen is number of bytes per record. If
the mode is omitted, then a random file is assumed.
The # is optional, as is the LEN specification.

(2) OPEN mode, # filenum, "filename", reclen

where the mode is "O" for output, "I" for input, "R"
for random access. The # and reclen are optional.

```
100   OPEN "FILE1" FOR OUTPUT AS #1 LEN =
      128
```

and

```
100   OPEN "O",#1,"FILE1",128
```

are equivalent to each other.

OPTION BASE   Declares the smallest value for an
array subscript. Must come before any DIM
statements.

```
10   OPTION BASE 1:DIM A(10)   'Makes subscript
                                range 1 to 10
```

OUT   Sends a single byte to an output port. Is
complementary to INP.

```
350   OUT 1000,34   'Sends 34 to output port 100
```

PEEK Returns the byte read from specified memory location, the number of which must be in range 0 to 65535.

```
600   K = PEEK(6000)    'Stores the byte found in
                         location 6000 in K
```

POKE Writes one byte to memory location specified.

```
450   POKE &H6B00,&HAA    'Places the
                          hexadecimal number
                          AA into the location
                          with hex address 6B00
```

POS Returns the current column of the cursor.

```
600   IF POS(0)>70 THEN CHR$(13)
         'Issues "carriage return" code when the cursor
          passes col. 70
```

PRINT or PRINT USING Outputs data to the screen.

```
 10   PRINT "HELLO SAILOR!"
500   P=23.45
510   PRINT USING "###.####";P    'Prints
                                   23.4500
```

PRINT# and PRINT#, USING As above, but prints to a specified file.

```
300   PRINT#2,A$,B$
310   PRINT#3,USING "###.####";P
```

PUT Places the contents of the random file buffer in the specified record of the file.

```
40   FIELD #2,2 AS I$,4 AS S$,8 AS D$
50   INPUT I,S,D
60   LSET I$=MKI$(I)
70   LSET S$=MKS$(S)
80   LSET D$=MKD$(D)
90   PUT #2,1
```

RANDOMIZE Sets the random number generator going. Needs an argument (between −32768 and 32767) to seed the generator. This needs to be used before RND.

```
50   RANDOMIZE (600)
```

READ Reads values, numeric or string, from a DATA line.

```
10   READ A$,B,C$
```

REM Remark statement ignored by the BASIC interpreter. Can be replaced by a single quote symbol. REM statements can be branched to.

```
10   REM THIS IS A REMARK
20   'SO IS THIS
```

RENUM Renumbers lines of a program.

```
RENUM 500,200,5    'Renumbers the program lines
                    from 500 onward so that they
                    start at 200 and increment in
                    units of 5
```

The default values are 10 for the first parameter, the first program line for the second and 10 for the third.

RESET   Closes down all open files and clears the system buffer. Effectively the same as CLOSE.

RESTORE   After reading from a DATA line the pointer can be returned to an earlier line number allowing the data to be reread.

500   RESTORE 300   'Returns the pointer to line 300

The default value is the first line of DATA.

RESUME   Resumes program execution after an error recovery has taken place.

100   RESUME 0   'Resumes at line where error
                   occurred. The 0 is optional
120   RESUME NEXT   'Resumes at line after the
                      error
140   RESUME 190   'Resumes at line 190

RETURN   Transfers control from a subroutine to the instruction following the GOSUB instruction.

5000   'SUBROUTINE STARTS HERE
5900   RETURN 'RETURNS CONTROL TO MAIN
        PROGRAM

RIGHT$ Returns the rightmost n characters from a string.

500   D$=RIGHT$(A$,5)   'Stores the rightmost 5
                          characters of A$ in D$

RND Returns a random number in the range 0 to 1. To generate random integers in the range 0 through n you need INT(RND*(n+1)). This must be preceded by RANDOMIZE.

RSET As LSET but right-justifies in the buffer field.

RUN Executes a BASIC program from a specified line number.

```
RUN 500     'Starts execution at line 500. If the line
             number is omitted the default is the
             lowest number line
RUN "PROG1",R 'Loads and runs the program
             PROG1. The optional R switch
             leaves any data files open when
             the program terminates
```

SAVE Saves the current program in memory to disk under the specified name.

```
SAVE "PROG2"    'Saves under the name of PROG2
SAVE "PROG2",A  'Saves the program in ASCII
                 format
SAVE "PROG2",P
    'Saves the program such that it cannot be listed
     or edited. A program saved like this cannot be
     unprotected
```

SGN Returns the sign (+ or −) of the argument. If positive 1 is returned. If negative −1 is returned and if zero 0 is returned.

```
670   P=−10
675   K=SGN(P)   'Stores −1 in K
```

SIN   The trigonometric sine function. The argument
must be in radians, not degrees.

```
500   X=1.2
510   S=SIN(X)   'Stores .9320391 in S
```

SPACE$ Returns a string filled with spaces.

```
300   F$=SPACE$(20)   'Stores 20 spaces in F$
```

SPC   Causes the printer head or the cursor to skip a
specified number of spaces.

```
700   PRINT "HELLO";SPC(5);"SAILOR"
          'Leaves 5 spaces between the words
```

SQR   Evaluates the square root of the argument.

```
200   X=45.78
210   Y=SQR(X)   'Stores 6.766092 in Y
```

STOP   Terminates the execution of your program.
Does not close any files; END does. You can
continue with CONT.

STR$ Assigns the string representation of a numeric
variable to a string variable.

```
35   X=5.78
40   X$=STR$(X)   'Stores "5.78" in X$
```

STRING$ Produces a string of n specified
characters.

```
300   A$=STRING$(10,"*")   'Stores a string of 10
                                "*" characters in A$
```

SWAP   Will exchange the values of two variables.

600   SWAP P,Q   'Exchanges the values of P and Q

is the equivalent of:

600   T=P:P=Q:Q=T

TAB   Tabs printer or screen cursor n spaces.

650   PRINT TAB(25);"HELLO"
660   'Prints the characters starting in the 25th
       column

TAN   The trigonometric tangent of the argument

60   X=0.5
65   T=TAN(0.5)   'Stores 0.5463025 in T

TIME$ Used for setting or retrieving the current
time. The time is held in a string of eight characters of
the form "HH:MM:SS". The time may have been set
from within MS-DOS and can be accessed from
BASIC, as with DATE$.

10   PRINT TIME$
20   INPUT T$ 'T$ could be "12:00:00" or "12:00"
30   TIME$=T$

TRON   Sets the trace function on. Displays each line
number as it is executed.

TROFF   Sets the trace function off.

USR   Calls a machine code subroutine and passes a specified argument to it.

```
700  DEF USR3=&HA000    'Defines the start
                          address of the
                          subroutine
710  F=USR3(10)         'Passes the argument in
                          brackets to USR3 and stores
                          the result in F
```

VAL   Converts a string variable into its numerical equivalent. If the first character of the string is non-numeric, 0 is returned.

```
200  V=VAL("567.8")    'Stores 567.8 in V
```

VARPTR   Returns the memory address of a variable or file control block.

```
300  V=VARPTR(LIST(0))   'Passes the address of
                           the lowest element of
                           the list LIST to V
400  V=VARPTR(#3)        'Passes the starting address
                           of the file control block for
                           file #3 to V
```

VARPTR is only applicable to disk files.

WAIT   Holds up program execution while examining the status of an input port.

```
500  WAIT 64,5
       'Holds up execution until port 64 receives a bit
        in position 5
```

WHILE/WEND   A looping instruction executed 'while' a condition holds.

```
100   R$="YES"              Note that the value of R$
110   WHILE R$="YES"        has to be 'seeded' with
120   INPUT X               'YES' otherwise the loop
130   T=T+X                 will never be entered at all
140   INPUT R$
150   WEND
160   PRINT T
```

WIDTH   Defines the number of characters in an output line.

```
10   WIDTH 40   'Sets screen width to 40 characters
```

WRITE   Outputs characters to screen separating them with commas and enclosing string constants in quotes. (Similar to PRINT)

WRITE#   Outputs data to a serial file. Unlike PRINT# it places commas between the variables in the file and encloses string constants in quotes.

Personal BASIC

This version of BASIC is supplied with the CP/M-86 operating systems and is designed to help a programmer new to the BASIC language to write programs. The more usual version of the language waits until execution time before it scans each line of program for syntax errors. Personal BASIC does this as each line is entered. The message

60

Something is wrong

is displayed as soon as a line with an error is
entered. A small up-arrow, ^, is placed under the
line at approximately the point where the error has
occurred. If an instruction causing a jump to a line
number which does not exist is entered then, when
the program is run, a message saying

Line number does not exist at line nn
Program not run

is displayed.

The error messages are fairly rudimentary but
certainly stop the programmer entering obvious
rubbish. The program itself is kept in a text file called
"BASIC.WRK" and so can be edited by any text
editor if required.

Graphics package

In order to display the sophisticated graphics
available on the Apricot you first of all have to load
the GSX-86 graphics system extension. This is done
by typing:

A>GSXBAS

followed by:

A>GRAPHICS

then you can type MSBASIC and you will be able to
use the graphics package with the BASIC language
interpreter. To see how this package works and
some of the facilities available, you should load and
run the BASIC program called "GSXDEMO1".

This will serve as a short, but useful, introduction to Apricot graphics. However, if you wish to discover all the features of the GSX graphics package supplied with your Apricot you will find that you need to purchase the GSX manual from ACT. This will give you all the instructions on the use of this package.

SuperCalc

SuperCalc (TM)* is a versatile spreadsheet program which is ideally suited for handling such activities as financial planning, maintenance of price lists and catalogues and anything where complex calculations are required in the 'what would we have if we did . . .?' situation. A full description of SuperCalc is to be found in the Pitman *Handbook of SuperCalc*. What follows is a brief outline of some of the facilities it offers.

SuperCalc is loaded on the Apricot either by selection via a ladder from the manager or directly from the operating system by typing:

A>SC

The first thing you will see is the copyright notice followed by the instruction to press the Return key in order to get started.

Then a blank spreadsheet is displayed on the screen. As you can see it consists of a series of columns headed A–H and a series of rows numbered 1–20. The top left-hand cell is highlighted and there are three lines of information at the bottom of the screen:

*SuperCalc is a registered trademark of Sorcim Corp.

```
      | A ‖  B ‖  C ‖  D ‖  E ‖  F ‖  G ‖  H |
 1  | <   >
 2  |
 3  |
 4  |
 5  |
 6  |
 7  |
 8  |
 9  |
10  |
11  |
12  |
13  |
14  |
15  |
16  |
17  |
18  |
19  |
20  |
>A1
Width: 9   Memory:33   Last Cell:A1   ? for HELP
 1>
```

The last three lines on the screen record the status of
your spreadsheet. The first of these tells you the
reference of the current cell, that is the one
highlighted. In this case it is cell A1. When you move
the highlight to any one of the cells of the
spreadsheet, its contents are displayed on this line.
You move from cell to cell, by the way, by using the
arrow keys. The > in front of the A1 tells you in which
direction the highlight will move if you press the
Return key. The symbols used are:

>	Right
<	Left
^	Up
v	Down

Under the Display Line is the Prompt Line. At present it gives you information regarding the number of characters displayed in each cell, which can be changed, how much memory is left for storing the current spreadsheet and the reference of the last cell visited. The amount of memory reduces as you enter data into the sheet. The Prompt Line is also used for other information, as you will see later. The bottom line is known as the Entry Line and anything you type in from now onward is displayed on this line. The number on the Entry Line tells you the current cursor position for the entry you are making. As each character is typed in, this number increments.

What you are seeing is, in fact, only a small portion of a very much larger sheet. The complete sheet contains 254 rows and 63 columns. The columns are lettered from A to Z, AA to AZ and then BA to BK. The arrow keys allow you to move around the sheet, vertically and horizontally. The reference for the cell where the highlight is always displayed on the top Status Line, together with the symbol which shows the direction in which the highlight last moved. You can move around the screen much faster if you know the cell reference you are aiming to reach. An 'express' way of moving about is to press the '=' key. Press = and enter **BK254** and you will get this:

```
   | A ‖ B ‖ C ‖ D ‖ E ‖ F ‖ G ‖ H |
 1 | <   >
 2 |
 3 |
 4 |
 5 |
 6 |
 7 |
 8 |
 9 |
10 |
11 |
12 |
13 |
14 |
15 |
16 |
17 |
18 |
19 |
20 |
>A1
Enter cell to jump to.
3>=>BK254
```

As soon as you press the Return key, you will get this:

```
        | BD || BE || BF || BG || BH || BI || BJ || BK |
235  |
236  |
237  |
238  |
239  |
240  |
241  |
242  |
243  |
244  |
245  |
246  |
247  |
248  |
249  |
250  |
251  |
252  |
253  |
254  |                                              <    >
>BK254
Width: 9   Memory:33   Last Cell:A1   ? for HELP
  1>
```

Repeat the operation by pressing = followed by
A1 and you will get back to the start.

As a very simple example of what the spreadsheet
will do we can use it to produce a simple shopping
list. For this we need to list a number of articles, how
much each costs, how many of each we require and
get the spreadsheet to calculate the cost of the
individual items and their grand total. First of all we
will have to enter the names of the articles to be

66

bought. This is done very simply by typing the names of the goods in column A. In order to do this we type them in but preceded with a double quotation mark, **"**. This tells SuperCalc that we are entering names and not cell references or formulae. We proceed down the column using the downward arrow key until we have this:

```
    | A || B || C || D || E || F || G || H |
 1  | Milk
 2  | Coffee
 3  | Sugar
 4  | Bread
 5  | Biscuits
 6  | Cake
 7  | Butter
 8  | Soap
 9  | Cheese
10  | Jam
11  | <    >
12  |
13  |
14  |
15  |
16  |
17  |
18  |
19  |
20  |
vA11
Width: 9   Memory:33   Last Col/Row A10   ? for HELP
  1>
```

Then we go to column B and enter the number of
each item in our shopping list — 'how many' — and
we get this:

```
      | A || B || C || D || E || F || G || H |
 1  | Milk       2
 2  | Coffee     1
 3  | Sugar      1
 4  | Bread      2
 5  | Biscuits   3
 6  | Cake       1
 7  | Butter     2
 8  | Soap       3
 9  | Cheese     1
10  | Jam        3
11  |       <    >
12  |
13  |
14  |
15  |
16  |
17  |
18  |
19  |
20  |
vB11
Width: 9   Memory:33   Last Col/Row B10   ? for HELP
 1>
```

Next we have to enter the cost of each item in the appropriate rows of column C:

	A	B	C	D	E	F	G	H
1	Milk	2	.22					
2	Coffee	1	1.55					
3	Sugar	1	.66					
4	Bread	2	.42					
5	Biscuits	3	.55					
6	Cake	1	1.22					
7	Butter	2	.48					
8	Soap	3	.35					
9	Cheese	1	.98					
10	Jam	3	.45					
11			< >					
12								
13								
14								
15								
16								
17								
18								
19								
20								

vC11

Width: 9   Memory:33   Last Col/Row C10   ? for HELP

1>

So now we have 'how many' and 'how much' for each item in our shopping list. In order to calculate the cost, for example, of 2 pints of milk at 22 pence each we have to multiply 'how many' by 'how much'. We do this in SuperCalc by moving the highlight to the cell where we want the answer to appear. Then the 'formula' for calculating the total cost is entered.

In this case we move the highlight to cell D1 and type in **B1∗C1**:

```
     | A  || B  || C  || D  || E  || F  || G  || H  |
 1  | Milk       2    .22<    >
 2  | Coffee     1   1.55
 3  | Sugar      1    .66
 4  | Bread      2    .42
 5  | Biscuits   3    .55
 6  | Cake       1   1.22
 7  | Butter     2    .48
 8  | Soap       3    .35
 9  | Cheese     1    .98
10  | Jam        3    .45
11  |
12  |
13  |
14  |
15  |
16  |
17  |
18  |
19  |
20  |
>D1
Width: 9   Memory:33   Last Col/Row C10   ? for HELP
  1>B1∗C1
```

and when the Return key has been pressed we will
see:

```
      | A || B || C || D || E || F || G || H |
 1  | Milk        2    .22    .44
 2  | Coffee      1   1.55
 3  | Sugar       1    .66
 4  | Bread       2    .42
 5  | Biscuits    3    .55
 6  | Cake        1   1.22
 7  | Butter      2    .48
 8  | Soap        3    .35
 9  | Cheese      1    .98
10  | Jam         3    .45
11  |
12  |
13  |
14  |
15  |
16  |
17  |
18  |
19  |
20  |
>D1    Form=B1*C1
Width: 9   Memory:33   Last Col/Row C10   ? for HELP
  1>
```

71

This formula can be repeated down the column by entering B2∗C2 in cell D2, B3∗C3 in cell D3 and so on. Then we will have this:

```
      | A ||  B ||  C ||  D ||  E ||  F ||  G ||  H |
 1  | Milk       2    .22    .44
 2  | Coffee     1   1.55   1.55
 3  | Sugar      1    .66    .66
 4  | Bread      2    .42    .84
 5  | Biscuits   3    .55   1.65
 6  | Cake       1   1.22   1.22
 7  | Butter     2    .48    .96
 8  | Soap       3    .35   1.05
 9  | Cheese     1    .98    .98
10  | Jam        3    .45   1.35
11  |                        <     >
12  |
13  |
14  |
15  |
16  |
17  |
18  |
19  |
20  |
vD11
Width: 9   Memory:33   Last Col/Row D10   ? for HELP
 1>
```

All that remains for us to do is to calculate the total bill, which is found by totalling all the entries in column D. There are two ways of doing this. One is that we could enter the formula:

D1+D2+D3+D4+D5+D6+D7+D8+D9+D10

into cell D11. This will work, but is rather longwinded. Alternatively, we could type:

SUM(D1:D10)

instead. This says 'calculate the sum of all the numbers in cells D1 to D10'. In either case, we will get this:

	A	B	C	D	E	F	G	H
1	Milk	2	.22	.44				
2	Coffee	1	1.55	1.55				
3	Sugar	1	.66	.66				
4	Bread	2	.42	.84				
5	Biscuits	3	.55	1.65				
6	Cake	1	1.22	1.22				
7	Butter	2	.48	.96				
8	Soap	3	.35	1.05				
9	Cheese	1	.98	.98				
10	Jam	3	.45	1.35				
11				10.7				
12				< >				
13								
14								
15								
16								
17								
18								
19								
20								

vD12
Width: 9   Memory:33   Last Col/Row D11   ? for HELP
  1>

The actual entries in our spreadsheet look like this:

	A		B		C		D		E		F		G		H	
1	Milk	2			.22		B1*C1								
2	Coffee	1			1.55		B2*C2								
3	Sugar	1			.66		B3*C3								
4	Bread	2			.42		B4*C4								
5	Biscuits	3			.55		B5*C5								
6	Cake	1			1.22		B6*C6								
7	Butter	2			.48		B7*C7								
8	Soap	3			.35		B8*C8								
9	Cheese	1			.98		B9*C9								
10	Jam	3			.45		B10*C10								
11							SUM(D1:D10)								
12							< >								
13															
14															
15															
16															
17															
18															
19															
20															

vD12

Width: 9   Memory:33   Last Col/Row D11   ? for HELP

1>

The way we can display the formulae as shown above, instead of the numbers, is described in the Pitman *Handbook of SuperCalc*.

Finally, we can change any of the entries in columns B or C and immediately get the entire bill recalculated to take the change into account. For example, if we want to change the number of packets of biscuits to 4 we only have to move the highlight to cell B5 and type 4 and we immediately get this:

	A ||| B	|| C	|| D	|| E	|| F	|| G	|| H
1	Milk	2	.22	.44				
2	Coffee	1	1.55	1.55				
3	Sugar	1	.66	.66				
4	Bread	2	.42	.84				
5	Biscuits	4	.55	2.2				
6	Cake <	>	1.22	1.22				
7	Butter	2	.48	.96				
8	Soap	3	.35	1.05				
9	Cheese	1	.98	.98				
10	Jam	3	.45	1.35				
11				11.25				
12								
13								
14								
15								
16								
17								
18								
19								
20								

vB6   Form = 1
Width: 9   Memory:33   Last Col/Row D11   ? for HELP
 1>

So much for the way that SuperCalc works for us. There is, however, rather more to it than just that. There are a range of commands which enable us to control the spreadsheet and the way it looks. You can save a spreadsheet on disk, load an existing spreadsheet for modification, control the format of the cells which contain the information, print the spreadsheet on our printer and so on. SuperCalc commands are initiated by pressing '/' key and on the Prompt Line you get a list of available commands:

	A	B	C	D	E	F	G	H
1	Milk	2	.22	.44				
2	Coffee	1	1.55	1.55				
3	Sugar	1	.66	.66				
4	Bread	2	.42	.84				
5	Biscuits	3	.55	1.65				
6	Cake	1	1.22	1.22				
7	Butter	2	.48	.96				
8	Soap	3	.35	1.05				
9	Cheese	1	.98	.98				
10	Jam	3	.45	1.35				
11				10.7				
12			< >					
13								
14								
15								
16								
17								
18								
19								
20								

vD12
Enter B,C,D,E,F,G,I,L,M,O,P,Q,R,S,T,U,W,Z or ?
2>/

You then have to enter one of the command letters and SuperCalc will supply the whole word which it stands for. For example, if you press L the word 'Load' appears on the Entry Line and the Prompt Line changes to a prompt which asks you the name of the file you wish to load. Press S and the word 'Save' appears and the Prompt Line asks you for the name you wish to give the spreadsheet when it is saved on disk.

The command letters have the following effects:

Letter	Effect
B	Enters a blank in a cell
C	Copy a cell, part of a row or column, or a block to another part of the spreadsheet
D	Delete a column or row
E	Edit an entry
F	Format a cell, row, column or whole spreadsheet
G	Global — Set worksheet options
I	Insert a new row or column
L	Load a named spreadsheet from disk
M	Move a column or row to a new location
O	Output a spreadsheet to disk or printer
P	Protect the contents of a cell from being overwritten
Q	Quit — Leave SuperCalc
R	Replicate a cell or group of cells into another part of the spreadsheet. Useful for copying formulae

Letter	Effect
S	Save the current spreadsheet under a unique name on disk
T	Place fixed titles on the spreadsheet
U	Unsave — Remove protection from cells
W	Split the display into two separate windows
Z	Zap (clear) the entire spreadsheet
?	Produces the HELP messages

SuperCalc arithmetic functions available are:

Function	Effect
SUM	Sums the contents of a range of cells.
	SUM(A1:J1), SUM(A1,D5*5,F1,H10:H30)
COUNT	Counts the number of non-empty cells in a specified range.
	COUNT(B1:B50)
AVERAGE	Calculates the average of the entries in a range of cells.
	AVERAGE(A1:A20) AVERAGE(J1,J3,J5,J10:J20,J30*10)
MIN	Returns the smallest entry held in a range of cells.
	MIN(A1:A50)

Function	Effect
MAX	Returns the largest entry in a range of cells.
	MAX(A1:A50)
INT	Returns the integer part of the number in a specified cell.
	INT(H4) INT(G23/10)
ABS	Returns the absolute value of the number in a specified cell.
	ABS(J3*J4)
SIN	Returns the sine function of the entry in a specified cell.
	SIN(D3)
COS	As above for cosine.
	COS(P4*P5)
TAN	As above for tangent.
	TAN(J12)
ASIN	Returns the arcsine function for the entry in a specified cell.
	ASIN(A4)
ATAN	As above for arctan.
	ATAN(D3+F3)

Function	Effect
EXP	Returns the exponential function of the contents of a specified cell.
	EXP(G3*F3)
SQRT	Returns the square root of the contents of a specified cell.
	SQRT(F3)
	SQRT(SUM(A5^2+A6^2)
LN	Returns the natural logarithm of the contents of a specified cell.
	LN(D4)
LOG10	Returns the logarithm to the base 10 of the contents of a specified cell.
	LOG10(T5)
PI	Returns the numerical value of pi to 16 significant digits.
	PI
IF, OR, AND, NOT	Logical tests.
	IF(A4>A5,B4,B5)
	OR(A6,A7)
	AND(A6,A7)
	NOT(F5)
LOOKUP	Looks up a value in a table.
	LOOKUP(F5,D1:D25)

Function	Effect
NPV	Evaluates the net present value of a set of cash returns at a specified discount.
	NPV(A4,B1:B12)
ERROR	Displays ERROR in the cell.
	ERROR
NA	Displays NA, 'Not Available', in the cell.
	NA

A full explanation of how the above commands and functions are used is given in the Pitman *Handbook for SuperCalc*.

SuperPlanner

SuperPlanner (TM)* is described as a 'personal organization tool'. It is a combination of diary, address book and card index. SuperPlanner is accessed via a ladder from the manager or directly from MS-DOS by typing:

A>SPLAN

SuperPlanner's main menu offers you five options, each one displayed over a touch-sensitive key on the Microscreen. They are:

ADDRESS, CALENDAR, CARD BOX, REMINDERS, FILES

*SuperPlanner is a registered trademark of Sorcim Corp.

Press the appropriate key and you enter the facility chosen.

ADDRESS   This displays the addresses, which are stored in alphabetical order of the first word on the first line of each entry. You can flip through the address file by using the arrow keys. A typical page from the address file would be:

11/10/84	ADDRESS BOOK	11:45
NAME/PHONE	ADDRESS	
Green, Steve	Midland Micro Services	
(0780-53477)	31 Broad Street	
	Stamford	

Turner, Brian	CETAS Consultants Ltd	
(0406-24900)	12/14 West End	
	Holbeach Lincs PE12 7LW	

To move through the Address Book the arrow keys are used as follows:

SHIFT and ↑	Next page
SHIFT and ↓	Previous page
SHIFT and ←	First page
SHIFT and →	Last page
↑	Line up
↓	Line down
←	Field left
→	Field right

The options available from ADDRESS are:

ADD, EDIT, DELETE, SLCT/find, PRINT, S/PAD

CALENDAR   This displays the calendar for the current month with any days which have an activity scheduled marked with an asterisk:

	SUN	MON	TUES	WED	THURS	FRI	SAT
					1	2	3
NOVEMBER	4	5	6*	7*	8*	9	10
1984	11	12	13	14	15*	16	17
	18	19	20*	21	22*	23	24
	25	26*	27	28	29	30	

You can move through the calendar by using the arrow key as follows:

↓	Moves one week forward
↑	Moves one week back
←	Moves back one day
→	Moves forward one day

In conjunction with the SHIFT key, these movements become:

↓	One month ahead
↑	One month back
←	January of this year
→	December of this year

The options available from CALENDAR are:

NEW DATE, ACTIVITIES, REMINDER

CARD-BOX   This is a computerized card index of notes on topics chosen by yourself. Again, the entries in the Card-Box file are stored in alphabetical order based on the first twelve characters of the first line of each entry. As with the Address file, you can flip through the Card-Box using the arrow keys.

The first field of each entry is shown enclosed within brackets and can be used as an identifier for that entry. A typical screen from Card-Box might look like this:

11/10/84   CARD BOX   11:50
   INDEX   NOTES

   (PITHDBKAPRCT)
   PITMAN PUBLISHING
   CONTRACT ISSUED — 20TH OCT 84 —
      ADVANCE PD 25TH OCT 84
   STARTED — 1ST NOV 84
   WORK IN PROGRESS — DELIVERY DATE
      — 31ST DEC 84

To flip through the Card Box, use the arrow keys:

Shift and ←   First page
Shift and →   Last page
Shift and ↑   Previous page
Shift and ↓   Next page

The options available from CARD BOX are:

ADD, EDIT, DELETE, SLCT/find, PRINT, S/PAD

REMINDERS   This displays those entries in the Activities file which have been specially marked with the ! character, irrespective of the date of the activity.

FILES   This allows you to erase, copy, rename, display the screen or print any file in the directory. It is another way into the MS-DOS utilities of ERAse, COPY, REName, TYPE or TYPE with the print toggle (^P) on. The three files kept by SuperPlanner are called ADDRESS.DAT, CARDBOX.DAT and ACTIVITY.DAT.

The scratch pad

The scratch pad is a temporary file onto which data, addresses, activities or notes from the card box can be placed prior to transfer to another one of the SuperPlanner files.

Options from CALENDAR

NEW DATE   If NEW DATE is selected you have the facility to enter a date so that the calendar for the month of that date is displayed with the cursor positioned at the day entered. Note that the date must be entered in American format: MM-DD-YY.

ACTIVITIES   By moving the cursor to any one of the dates on the calendar and pressing ACTIVITIES, or Return, the activities recorded for that day are displayed. A typical Activities screen would look like this:

11/14/84 Activities for Wednesday,
November 14 1984   **3:15**
!   9:30   See builder regarding screeding
of kitchen floor
A 10.30   Telephone ACT re use of CP/M
on hard disk Apricot
!   2:30   Dental appointment
E   Pay for bathroom fittings

Note that the times should be given in twenty-four
hour clock notation. Early versions of SuperPlanner
allow you to use AM and PM. The latest versions do
not.

The first field for each Activity has an optional
code. The ! symbol is the reminder symbol which
causes that entry to be displayed when the reminder
option is chosen from the calendar. The A code is
there to cause an audible alarm to sound at the
specified time, 10.30 in this example.

The other codes can be chosen for their
significance to you from the letters B–Z. For
example, the code E could stand for an expense.
The description of each activity is restricted
to 60 characters.

REMINDER   If this option is chosen, all those
activities marked with the ! character are listed,
irrespective of date.

Options from ADDRESS

ADD   You are allowed to have five entry lines in each Address record. The first is the name which can contain up to 25 characters. Remember that this is going to act as a sort key, so decide whether you want names stored in surname order, first-name order or in some other. Starting each Mr, Mrs or Ms will have rather unpredictable results! The second field is the telephone number and can include slashes or dashes as required. The three address lines can contain up to 52 characters each, including commas. There are three options from this screen:

MARK BLK, COPY BLK, ADD NEXT

The first of these allows you to mark the beginning of a field on the screen which, when this option is chosen, moves the block into the buffer. COPY BLK will bring the contents of the buffer onto the screen at the current cursor position. ADD NEXT places the newly entered address into its proper place on the Address Book file.

EDIT   Once an address has been entered it can be edited to allow for changes in address or status. You may first search for the entry to be changed by pressing SHIFT and SLCT/find. Then you can enter up to 20 characters which occur in the entry you are looking for. Press the Return key and the first entry to contain those letters anywhere in the entry will be displayed. If it is not the one you want you can repeat the operation and SuperPlanner will look for the next entry to contain that key.

On reaching the required entry press EDIT and using the arrow keys move the cursor to the part of the entry you wish to change. You can now insert or delete characters by using the following sequences:

Keys	Effect
Control-B	Move to end of file
Control-C	Forward one page
Control-D	Right cursor
Control-E	Up cursor
Control-F	Right word
Control-G	Delete character under cursor
Control-N	Delete to end of line
Control-O	Insert mode on/off toggle
Control-R	Back one page
Control-S	Left cursor
Control-T	Move to top of file
Control-X	Down cursor
DEL	Delete character to left of cursor

When editing is finished you press the FINISH key.

While in EDIT or ADD you have a choice of the two options MARK BLK and COPY BLK. The first of these allows you to mark a section of the current screen up to 80 characters long and place into a buffer. Then when you display a screen into which you wish to copy the stored text you select its EDIT mode and press COPY BLK. The block of characters stored in the buffer are then inserted into the new screen at the selected point. The original text is unaltered and so are the contents of the buffer, so the same piece of text can be placed in several parts of the SuperPlanner system. The contents of the buffer remain unaltered until a new MARK BLK is issued.

SLCT/find   Will produce the SELECT screen which looks like this:

11/15/84	**ADDRESS BOOK**	10:34
name from:		**to:**
phone from:		**to:**
address line 1 from:		**to:**
address line 2 from:		**to:**
address line 3 from:		**to:**

This screen offers you two options: SELECT ON and ZAP. SELECT is in fact a toggle switching SELECT on or off. Switching this OFF retains the selection criteria but allows you to flip through other addresses. ZAP erases the current selection criteria.

If SELECT is switched ON you can enter ranges of selection for each of the lines of the address. Using 'wildcards' allows you considerable flexibility in this selection. The wildcards are the * symbol and the ? symbol.

Placing a * before or after a string of characters is like saying 'any set of characters'. So that a name entered as "SMITH*" would account for names like "SMITH", "SMITHERS" and "SMITHERINGALE". A name entered as "*DER" would account for names like "LANDER", "CALLENDER" and so on. If you entered "*OO*", then all names which contained the 'OO' characters anywhere would be selected.

The ? symbol replaces only a single character so that '4??' stands for any three characters starting with the digit 4.

If our selection screen looks like this:

11/15/84	**ADDRESS BOOK**	10:34

name from: A∗   **to: G∗**
   phone from: **to:**
address line 1 from: **to:**
address line 2 from:∗CARDIFF∗   **to:**
address line 3 from: **to:**

we will select all those addresses for names starting
with the letters A through G who contain the word
'CARDIFF' in the second line of the address. If you
press the FINISH key, having first of all pressed
SELECT ON, you will see all your selected entries
displayed.

DELETE   You can delete complete entries or
portions of entries in the Address Book. When
DELETE is chosen you are presented with three
options: RECORD deletes the address containing the
cursor; SELECTED deletes all addresses meeting
criteria already selected; and ALL deletes all the
addresses in the Address Book.

PRINT   Operates in the same way as DELETE except
that it prints the addresses instead of deleting them.

S-PAD   Allows you to transfer one or more
addresses between the Address Book and the
Scratch Pad. The screen will look like this:

11/16/84	**ADDRESS BOOK**	12:45

Transfer To or From Scratch Pad ?

   RECORD   SELECTED   ALL

The question is either answered with T or F — for 'To' or 'From'.

If **T** was entered followed by RECORD the record currently containing the cursor is moved to the Scratch Pad. If SELECTED was chosen, then all those records satisfying the criteria chosen by SELECT are transferred. If the Scratch Pad is not empty you will be asked if you wish to (A)ppend or (O)verwrite the records on the Scratch Pad. ALL moves all the addresses to the Scratch Pad.

If **F** was entered, then transfers from the Scratch Pad can be made. This causes a further question to be asked:

Start from Beginning of S-PAD Yes or No ?

To start the transfer answer **Y** and answer all the subsequent questions with **N** until the Scratch Pad is empty. Press FINISH after all the transfers have been made.

The options available from ACTIVITIES are the same as those from ADDRESS, namely:

ADD, EDIT, DELETE, SLCT/find, PRINT, S-PAD

The ADD option allows you to add a further activity to that day. EDIT allows you to change an entry. (The editing functions are the same as those for editing addresses.) DELETE allows you to delete any or all of the activities from that day. SLCT/find makes it possible for you to select all those activities which fulfil certain conditions. PRINT allows you to print out the current entry or all entries which have been selected. The only screen you cannot print is a Calendar screen.

If SLCT/find is chosen, then the SELECT screen is displayed. This looks like this:

09/14/84   ACTIVITY Selection SELECT OFF
3:55

date from:	**to:**
category from:	**to:**
time from:	**to:**
note from:	**to:**

The options available from this screen are the same as from the SELECT screen for ADDRESSES, namely:

SELECT, ZAP, MARK FLD, COPY FLD

You can then enter your criteria in the appropriate fields so that if you wanted to list all the telephone calls made to ACT between certain dates you would have a screen looking like this:

09/14/84   ACTIVITY Selection SELECT OFF
3:55

date from: 10/01/84	**to:10/30/84**
category from: A	**to:**
time from:	**to:**
note from: *ACT*	**to:**

The entry in the 'note' criterion is using the 'wildcard' feature, exactly as in the SELECT option in ADDRESSES, for saying 'any entry which contains the characters ACT'. When SELECT is pressed, the selection process begins and the appropriate activities are displayed.

ZAP clears all the current selection criteria and allows you to introduce some more if required.

MARK FLD and COPY FLD again work in the same way as MARK BLK and COPY BLK from the ADD screen from ADDRESSES.

Options from CARD BOX

These are exactly the same as the options offered from ADDRESS and ACTIVITIES. When using ADD to add a further entry into the Card Box the end of the first entry and the beginning of the second must be separated by depressing either the Tab key or the Return key. The second field takes up the rest of the screen and can occupy four lines. The SELECT screen looks like this:

11/15/84	**CARD BOX**	3:25
index:		**to:**
text line 1 from:		**to:**
text line 2 from:		**to:**
text line 3 from:		**to:**
text line 4 from:		**to:**

A selection of, say, all the Pitman books being worked on, could be made like this:

11/15/84	**CARD BOX**	3:25
index: PIT∗		**to:**
text line 1 from:		**to:**
text line 2 from:		**to:**
text line 3 from:		**to:**
text line 4 from: WORK IN PROGRESS∗		**to:**

The options offered by this screen are the same as those offered by the other SELECT screens.

SuperWriter

SuperWriter (TM)* is the word-processing package
supplied with your Apricot. It is liberally supplied
with help screens and menus to help the newcomer to
become familiar with a word processor.

SuperWriter is loaded either by selection from a
ladder in manager or by typing:

A>SW

if you are in the MS-DOS operating system. A screen
is first displayed with the usual copyright notice and
at the top of the screen a line which tells you the time
and the name of the current document being edited.
At first, of course, there is no document and so this
line shows:

A:IDLE.NO edit document

Beneath this is the main menu consisting of six
options, which can be chosen by either moving the
cursor to the required one or depressing the
appropriate touch-sensitive key beneath the
microscreen. The menu choices are:

EDIT, QUIT, PRINT, CHECK, DISK, UTILITIES

*SuperWriter is a registered trademark of Sorcim Corp.

At the bottom of the screen is a line which tells you that you depress the Space Bar to move the cursor, press Return to select your choice, press the Escape key to cancel a choice and press the ? key to get some help. This last key is known in SuperWriter as the AnswerKey*. If you choose the last of these options you are presented with the AnswerScreen*. This screen gives a brief outline of the functions of the various options as shown on the following page.

*AnswerKey and AnswerScreen are trademarks of Sorcim Corp.

SuperWriter 1.00 AnswerScreen Main Menu

EDIT	= Create or revise document – Correct spelling errors – Add formatting directives – Save a document on disk
QUIT	= End SuperWriter and return to System
PRINT	= Print formatted document – Print document "as is" – Print form letters or mailing lists
CHECK Spelling	= Find and mark all possible misspelled words
DISK Directory	= List of documents and document history
UTILITY	= Display or include document – Delete or rename documents – Spool document to printer (background printing) – Revise document history – Maintain Dictionaries – Call SuperCalc

Press any key to continue

EDIT commands

The commands available while editing is in progress
enable you to move the cursor about on the screen,
scroll through the document being edited, insert and
delete text, find and replace text, move blocks of text,
save the document and print it. Many of the cursor
movement commands are similar to those used in
SuperCalc and the WordStar word-processing
package.

Cursor movements

Up one line	Ctrl-E or ↑
Down one line	Ctrl-X or ↓
Left character	Ctrl-S or ←
Left word	Ctrl-A
Right character	Ctrl-D or →
Right word	Ctrl-F
Start of text	Ctrl-T
End of text	Ctrl-B
Back one screen	Ctrl-R
Forward one screen	Ctrl-C
Scroll one line forward	Ctrl-Z
Scroll one line backward	Ctrl-W
Beginning of line	HOME
End of line	Ctrl-U
To next tab stop	TAB

Deletion of text

Character at cursor	Ctrl-G
Rest of word	Ctrl-Y
Rest of line	Ctrl-N
Complete line	LINE DELETE CHAR/s
Character to left of cursor	LINE DELETE CHAR

Insertion of text

Change mode	Ctrl-O or MS-1
Blank	LINE INSERT CHAR
Line	LINE INSERT CHAR/s
Mark	MS-2
Tab	ESC Tab

Find/Replace

Find next mark	MS-3	(MS-1, MS-2, etc.
Find next spell mark	MS-6	refer to the touch-sensitive
Repeat find	MS-4	keys under the
Repeat replace	MS-5	microscreen)

Other options

Print text	Ctrl-P
Exit and Save	ESC S
Exit and Zap	ESC Z

Inserting new text

New text can be inserted at any point in one of four modes. These are:

Type-over mode   Allows overtyping as with a
                  conventional typewriter

Insert mode	The characters you type are inserted at the current cursor position
Auto-insert mode	Used for altering single words without having to go into Insert. Acts like Type-over but with Insert operating at the end of the word
Page insertion	This opens up a space within the document at the cursor position to allow you to type in several lines of new text. When this mode is turned off the blank following your new text is deleted and the following text is closed up

When SuperWriter is first started up it is always in Insert mode. To change to any other mode you press Ctrl-O followed by A for Auto-insert or P for Page insert. Ctrl-O followed by I acts as a 'toggle' and switches Insert mode to Type-over mode and vice versa. Text is automatically rejustified as new text is inserted.

To move a block of text
Mark the beginning and end of the text to be moved with ESC followed by /. Move the cursor to the new position of the text and press ESC M and B. The text will move from its old position to its new position and the block markers will be removed. Only two block markers are allowed in a text.

To copy a block of text, leaving the original text unaltered, mark the block as before. Move the cursor to the position required for the copy to start. Press ESC C and B. The block markers remain in position. To copy the marked block to a file on disk for future use, press ESC C and W.

If a block of text is to be inserted into your document from a file stored on disk, position the cursor at the point where the insertion is to be made and press ESC I followed by the name of the file to be copied from. It will then be inserted in the text at that point.

Finding text

To find a desired character string in the text, position the cursor before the text to be located and press ESC F followed by the string being searched for (up to 22 characters are allowed). If the Return character is being searched for this is entered as Ctrl- ^ . If you need to find certain marks in the text — spelling marks, formfeeds, block marks or control characters — press MS-3 followed by F to find a formfeed, S to find a spelling mark, / to find a block mark and ^ (char) to find a control character.

Replacing text

To search for a specified string and then replace it with another string, press ESC R followed by the string to be replaced. You are then prompted for the characters to replace your string.

Changing the case

Very often you have to alter the case of text you have already entered; upper case to lower case and vice versa. SuperWriter allows you to do this without the tedium of having to delete the offending characters and retype them in the capitals or lower case. First of all you have to move the cursor to the start of the text to be changed and type ESC N. Then:

C	Capitalizes the character under the cursor. All characters to the right of this letter are put into lower case
L	Puts all characters to right of cursor up to the end of the word into lower case
U	Puts all characters to right of cursor up to the end of the word into upper case
Return	Puts all characters from the cursor to the end of the line into lower case
A	Puts all characters from the cursor to the end of the line into upper case
ESC	Return to Edit

PRINT command

Printing controls are entered into the text following a Ctrl-P command at the point where the command is to become operative. The controls are:

B	Starts/stops boldface printing
C	Centres current line between margins
H	Starts a hanging indent at the next tab stop. Indents whole paragraph
P	Throws a new page
R	Right justifies the current line

U	Starts/stops underlining of text
Space	Insert a hard space
-	Hyphenate if needed at this point
<	Superscript text. Switched off by > or Return
>	Subscript text. Switched off by < or Return
ESC	Return to Edit

Embedded formatting-commands
These commands are placed within the text
temporarily to override the general layout of tab
stops. These commands are prefixed with a back-
slash, \. In case you may wish to alter this — you may
use back-slashes in your text — to some other
character which you are not otherwise using you can
change from the back-slash to, say, a # sign by

\ cmd#

This establishes a new embedded prefix. The
command is terminated by a comma, another
command, a Return or another \ character.

\IN+n	Moves left margin n characters to right
\IN−n	Moves left margin n characters to left
\IN 0	Cancel margin moves (indentation)
\PI n	Indents first n characters of each paragraph
\PI 0	Cancels paragraph indent command
\TAB n	Tabs to nth column
\LINE n	Start printing on line n
\SP n	Print n blank lines before printing next characters
\LEFT	Left justifies text

\RIGHT	Right justifies text
\JUST	Left and right justifies text
\CENTER	Centres text between margins
\UNB	Sets underlining with broken line
\UNS	Sets underlining with solid line
\LIT	Only breaks lines when the line length is exceeded. Does not wrap words
\LW n	Sets the line width to n characters
\TM n	Sets top margin to n lines
\BM n	Sets bottom margin to n lines
\LM n	Sets left margin to the nth character
\SP n	Sets line spacing to n lines
\HEADER	Specifies the layout, line by line, to be
LINE1	included at the head of every page
LINE2	
LINE3	
\HE	
\FOOTER	Specifies the layout, line by line, to be
\LINE1	included at the foot of every page
\LINE2	
\LINE3	
\FE	
\AP P1 P2 P3	Automatic page numbering in header or footer. P1 is either H (Header) or F (Footer). P2 is either R (Right justify) or C (Centre). P3 is the starting page number. (*Note:* You cannot use \AP and either \HEADER or \FOOTER.)
\%PAGE or \%P	Current page number. Used in header and footer commands
\CCH	Clear current header
\CCF	Clear current footer

\INSERT filename	Insert the named file at this point
\CPI n	Choose the printing pitch, n characters per inch
\H n	Move printer head by n increments after printing each character. An increment is usually 1/60 inch or 1/120 inch
\K n	Backspace second of the following two characters by n increments. Such a command would look like \K-12\u'' in order to produce ü
\LPI n	Print at n lines per inch
\V n	Move vertically by n increments usually 1/48 inch) after printing each line
\PROP ON	Print with proportional spacing
\PROP OFF	Switch off proportional spacing
\FORMFEED ON/OFF	Switches a formfeed (top of new page) on or off
\OUT	Allows you to send control codes to your printer. The decimal equivalents of the codes are listed after OUT
\GET	Causes SuperWriter to pause and prompt for you to type text in
\ :text	Prompt for previously "GET"ted text. (For example: **\GET** name prompts for a name and stores it. Every time **\:name** appears in the text the stored name is inserted)
\SET	Assigns or changes a text or numeric variable

\VSIZE n	Specifies that n variables can be used. The default number is 32
\FILE,Tn,filename	
	Read n variables from the named file
\DATA t1,t2,t3,t4	
	Assigns names to the fields in the file. Must come after the \FILE command
\IF comparison,command	
	Compare two expressions. If true, execute command following
\SKIP n	Skip n Return characters
\SKIP TO char	
	Skip to next occurrence of the specified character
\FF	Sets printer to top of page. Inserted at start of a document
\NP	Skip to top of new page
\CNPn	Skip to new page if there are fewer than n lines left to be printed on the current page after the current paragraph. This is a global command
\CPB n	As above, but for one page only
\NOTE	Displays a comment on the screen
\WAIT	Prints a message and waits for any key to be pressed
\SHOW	Display listed parameters on screen
\DV	Display variables
\DF	Display file
\DB	Display buffers
\CLS	Clear screen
\SETUP	Starts a block of directives at the start of a piece of text
\TEXT	Ends the block of directives

Global settings such as line length, word wrapping, tab settings and margins can be set from the main Edit screen by the ESC G command. The settings required are chosen from a menu.

When a document is to be printed, the Print screen details all the current format settings such as the position of the margins, line width, spacing, page length and the top and bottom margins. This screen also gives you control over the number of copies of the document to be printed, the page numbering and the choice of printing in proportional spacing if your printer allows it. In addition, you have the choice of displaying your document on the screen in the exact format in which it will be printed. You can also print the document without formatting it or save the formatted document on disk ready for printing at a later date, or for incorporation in another document.

CHECK commands

SuperWriter also contains a spelling checker which can be invoked from the main menu screen. A dictionary containing 20 000 words is supplied with SuperWriter and you can add extra words to this as necessary. In addition, new dictionaries can be created for specific applications.

The spelling checker is used to proofread a document and will provide you with a count of the number of words, the number of unique words and the number of words which cannot be found in the dictionary. You can then examine the mismatched words, which may be incorrect spellings or new words which you may wish to add into the dictionary. All the mismatched words are displayed one at a time and you can choose your action from one of six options. These are indicated by the letters:

M A I R S E

M   Mark a word in the document
A   Add the word to the dictionary
I   Ignore the word
R   Review the previous word
S   Start a quick review
E   Exit

If a word has been marked incorrectly, then the mark can be edited out. The quick review allows you to mark, ignore or add the mismatches to the dictionary without displaying the words. Alternatively, you may list the remaining mismatches or return to the word-by-word review.

DISK commands

If you select the DISK option from the main menu you will first of all be presented with information regarding the amount of space occupied by your current document: how many words, characters, lines, pages and the number of keystrokes you have made. From here you have three options:

List all documents in your directory
List a specified set of documents, using
    wildcard characters in the name
Show the history of your document

The third of these, the document history option, will
display the history of the listed documents and is
chosen prior to selecting the listing option. If this is
chosen you will be given the size of the document, its
author, date of creation and the date of the last
modification to the document.

UTILITIES commands

Four options are available if you choose UTILITIES
from the main menu. These are:

LIBRARY
DOCUMENT
DICTIONARY
SUPERCALC

The first of these allows you several choices:

To display any document you have created but does
    not allow you to edit it
To include a part of any document with the current
    document
Delete a document from the disk
Reset the disk
Rename a document
Place a document onto the spooler ready for
    background printing

The second allows you to amend a document's history.

The DICTIONARY option gives you the facility to maintain a dictionary used in conjunction with the spelling checker.

The last option gives you access to SuperCalc in order to create a spreadsheet which can then be included in your document.

Special 'Keyed' document files are used to store sections of text which are likely to be used regularly; legal phrases, specifications, descriptions and prices are examples of this. These are set up in special files with a unique 'key' to each of the sections. The key is entered by typing in the form-feed character, F6 F, followed by the key. Then follows a brief description and the text on the next line. When the keyed document is displayed on the screen the form-feed character appears as a ! sign. So a keyed document might look like this:

! 0901 Brackets ½ inch
      Brackets, half inch, $0.99
! 0902 Brackets 1 inch
      Brackets, 1 inch, $1.25
! 0903 Brackets, 1 ½ inch
      Brackets, 1 ½ inch, $1.54

The keys are 0901, 0902 and 0903 in this case. If the include option is chosen, then the cursor is positioned at the point where the text is to be inserted and ESC is pressed. This returns you to the main menu. Then the UTILITIES option is chosen from that and the LIBRARY option selected. From this option 'Include' is chosen and the name of the keyed file is entered. You can then type the required key in and SuperWriter searches for a form-feed followed by that key. You then have the chance to include the text referred to by that key in with your document at the current cursor position. So if you choose key 0902 you have the ability to insert the text:

Brackets, 1 inch, $1.25

into your document. If you only specify the key as 09, then the first key to start with 09 is found. You can then skip to the next key starting with those characters if you have failed to choose the correct one.

Index

112

Computer Handbooks

Languages

Assembly Language for the 8086 and 8088   Robert
   Erskine
C Language   Friedman Wagner-Dobler

Business Applications

VisiCalc   Peter Gosling

Microcomputers

The Apricot   Peter Gosling
The Sinclair QL   Guy Langdon and
   David Heckingbottom

Operating Systems

Introduction to Operating Systems
   Lawrence Blackburn and Marcus Taylor

Pocket Guides

Programming

Programming   John Shelley
BASIC   Roger Hunt
COBOL   Ray Welland
FORTH   Steven Vickers
FORTRAN   Philip Ridler
FORTRAN 77   Clive Page
LOGO   Boris Allan
Pascal   David Watt

Assembly Languages

Assembly Language for the 6502   Bob Bright
Assembly Language for the 8085   Noel Morris
Assembly Language for the MC 68000 Series
   Robert Erskine
Assembly Language for the Z80   Julian Ullmann

Microcomputers

Acorn Electron   Neil Cryer and Pat Cryer
Commodore 64   Boris Allan
Programming for the Apple   John Gray
Programming for the BBC Micro   Neil Cryer
   and Pat Cryer
Sinclair Spectrum   Steven Vickers
The IBM PC   Peter Gosling

116

Operating Systems

CP/M Lawrence Blackburn and Marcus Taylor
MS-DOS Val King and Dick Waller
PC-DOS Val King and Dick Waller
UNIX Lawrence Blackburn and Marcus Taylor

Word Processors

Introduction to Word Processing Maddie Labinger
IBM Displaywriter Jacquelyne A. Morison
Philips P5020 Peter Flewitt
Wang System 5 Maddie Labinger
WordStar Maddie Labinger